New Testament
Bible Stories for Preschoolers
Family Nights Tool Chest

Creating Lasting Impressions for the Next Generation!

Jim Weidmann and Kirk Weaver
with Kurt Bruner

Cook Communications

Heritage Builders

To Melvin and Lois Hodges,
parents, grandparents, and great-grandparents.
I learned from you that:
Jesus is alive and real;
the Christian faith is an everyday adventure;
and a spiritual heritage is a family treasure.
—*K.W.*

Chariot Victor Publishing
a division of Cook Communications Ministries, Colorado Springs, Colorado 80918
Cook Communications, Paris, Ontario
Kingsway Communcations, Eastbourne, England

HERITAGE BUILDERS®/FAMILY NIGHT TOOL CHEST—BIBLE STORIES FOR PRESCHOOLERS™
(NEW TESTAMENT)
© 1999 by Jim Weidmann, Kirk Weaver, and Kurt Bruner

First edition 1999

Edited by Steve Parolini
Design by Bill Gray
Cover and Interior Illustrations by Guy Wolek

ISBN 1-56476-776-0

Printed and bound in the United States of America
03 02 01 00   5 4 3 2

Heritage Builders/Family Night Tool Chest—Bible Stories for Preschoolers (New Testament) is a Heritage Builders® book. To contact Heritage Builders Association, send email to: Hbuilders@aol.com.

Contents

Family Nights for Preschoolers on New Testament Bible Stories

The Heritage Builders® Series

This resource was created as an outreach of the Heritage Builders Association—a network of families and churches committed to passing a strong heritage to the next generation. Designed to motivate and assist families as they become intentional about the heritage passing process, this series draws upon the collective wisdom of parents, grandparents, church leaders, and family life experts, in an effort to provide balanced, biblical parenting advice along with effective, practical tools for family living. For more information on the goals and work of Heritage Builders Association, please see page 113.

Kurt Bruner, M.A.
Executive Editor
Heritage Builders® Series

@ Introduction

There is toothpaste all over the plastic-covered table. Four young kids are having the time of their lives squeezing the paste out of the tube—trying to expunge every drop like Dad told them to. "Okay," says Dad, slapping a twenty-dollar bill onto the table. "The first person to get the toothpaste back into their tube gets this money!" Little hands begin working to shove the peppermint pile back into rolled-up tubes—with very limited success.

Jim is in the midst of a weekly routine in the Weidmann home when he and his wife spend time creating "impression points" with the kids. "We can't do it, Dad!" protests the youngest child.

"The Bible tells us that's just like your tongue. Once the words come out, it's impossible to get them back in. You need to be careful what you say because you may wish you could take it back." An unforgettable impression is made.

Impression points occur every day of our lives. Intentionally or not, we impress upon our children our values, preferences, beliefs, quirks, and concerns. It happens both through our talk and through our walk. When we do it right, we can turn them on to the things we believe. But when we do it wrong, we can turn them off to the values we most hope they will embrace. The goal is to find ways of making this reality work for us, rather than against us. How? By creating and capturing opportunities to impress upon the next generation our values and beliefs. In other words, through what we've labeled impression points.

The kids are all standing at the foot of the stairs. Jim is at the top of that same staircase. They wait eagerly for Dad's instructions.

"I'll take you to Baskin Robbins for ice cream if you can figure how to get up here." He has the attention of all four kids. "But there are a few rules. First, you can't touch the stairs. Second, you can't touch the railing. Now, begin!"

After several contemplative moments, the youngest speaks up. "That's impossible, Dad! How can we get to where you are without touching the stairs or the railing?"

After some disgruntled agreement from two of the other children, Jacob gets an idea. "Hey, Dad. Come down here." Jim walks down the stairs. "Now bend over while I get on your back. Okay, climb the stairs."

Bingo! Jim proceeds to parallel this simple game with how it is impossible to get to God on our own. But when we trust Christ's completed work on our behalf, we can get to heaven. A lasting impression is made. After a trip up the stairs on Dad's back, the whole gang piles into the minivan for a double scoop of mint-chip.

Six years ago, Jim and his wife Janet began setting aside time to intentionally impress upon the kids their values and beliefs through a weekly ritual called "family night." They play games, talk, study, and do the things which reinforce the importance of family and faith. It is during these times that they intentionally create these impression points with their kids. The impact? The kids are having fun and a heritage is being passed.

⊙ intentional or "oops"?

Sometimes, we accidentally impress the wrong things on our kids rather than intentionally impressing the right things. But there is an effective, easy way to change that. Routine family nights are a powerful tool for creating intentional impression points with our children.

The concept behind family nights is rooted in a biblical mandate summarized in Deuteronomy 6:5-9.

> *"Love the LORD your God with all your heart and with all your soul and with all your strength. These commandments that I give you today are to be upon your hearts. Impress them on your children."*
> ***How?***
> *"Talk about them when you sit at home and when you walk along the road, when you lie down and when you get up. Tie them as symbols on your hands and bind them on your foreheads. Write them on the doorframes of your houses and on your gates."*

In other words, we need to take advantage of every opportunity to impress our beliefs and values in the lives of our children. A growing network of parents are discovering family nights to be a highly effective, user-friendly approach to doing just that. As one father put it, "This has changed our entire family life." And another dad, "Our investment of time and energy into family nights has more eternal value than we may ever know." Why? Because they are intentionally teaching their children at the wisdom level, the level at which the children understand and can apply eternal truths.

☺ truth is a treasure

Two boys are running all over the house, carefully following the complex and challenging instructions spelled out on the "truth treasure map" they received moments ago. An earlier map contained a few rather simple instructions that were much easier to follow. But the "false treasure box" it lead to left something to be desired. It was empty. Boo Dad! They hope for a better result with map number two.

STEP ONE:

Walk sixteen paces into the front family room.

STEP TWO:

Spin around seven times, then walk down the stairs.

STEP THREE:

Run backwards to the other side of the room.

STEP FOUR:

Try and get around Dad and climb under the table.

You get the picture. The boys are laughing at themselves, complaining to Dad, and having a ball. After twenty minutes of treasure hunting they finally reach the elusive "truth treasure box." Little hands open the lid, hoping for a better result this time around. They aren't disappointed. The box contains a nice selection of their favorite candies. Yea Dad!

"Which map was easier to follow?" Dad asks.

"The first one," comes their response.

"Which one was better?"

"The second one. It led to a true treasure," says the oldest.

"That's just like life," Dad shares, "Sometimes it's easier to follow what is false. But it is always better to seek and follow what is true."

They read from Proverbs 2 about the hidden treasure of God's truth and end their time repeating tonight's jingle—"It's best for you to seek what's true." Then they indulge themselves with a mouthful of delicious candy!

☺ the power of family nights

The power of family nights is twofold. First, it creates a formal setting within which Dad and Mom can intentionally instill beliefs, values, or character qualities within their child. Rather than defer to the influence of peers and media, or abdicate character training to the school and church, parents create the opportunity to teach their children the things that matter most.

The second impact of family nights is perhaps even more significant than the first. Twenty to sixty minutes of formal fun and instruction can set up countless opportunities for informal reinforcement. These informal impression points do not have to be created, they just happen—at the dinner table, while driving in the car, while watching television, or any other parent/child time together. Once you have formally discussed a given family night topic, you and your children will naturally refer back to those principles during the routine dialogues of everyday life.

If the truth were known, many of us hated family devotions while growing up. We had them sporadically at best, usually whenever our parents were feeling particularly guilty. But that was fine, since the only thing worse was a trip to the dentist. Honestly, do we really think that is what God had in mind when He instructed us to teach our children? As an alternative, many parents are discovering family nights to be a wonderful complement to or replacement for family devotions as a means of passing their beliefs and values to the kids. In fact, many parents hear their kids ask at least three times per week:

"Can we have family night tonight?"

Music to Dad's and Mom's ears!

@ Keys to Effective Family Nights

There are several keys which should be incorporated into effective family nights.

MAKE IT FUN!

Enjoy yourself, and let the kids have a ball. They may not remember everything you say, but they will always cherish the times of laughter—and so will you.

KEEP IT SIMPLE!

The minute you become sophisticated or complicated, you've missed the whole point. Don't try to create deeply profound lessons. Just try to reinforce your values and beliefs in a simple, easy-to-understand manner. Read short passages, not long, drawn-out sections of Scripture. Remember: The goal is to keep it simple.

DON'T DOMINATE!

You want to pull them into the discovery process as much as possible. If you do all the talking, you've missed the mark. Ask questions, give assignments, invite participation in every way possible. They will learn more when you involve all of their senses and emotions.

GO WITH THE FLOW!

It's fine to start with a well-defined outline, but don't kill spontaneity by becoming overly structured. If an incident or question leads you in a different direction, great! Some of the best impression opportunities are completely unplanned and unexpected.

MIX IT UP!

Don't allow yourself to get into a rut or routine. Keep the sense of excitement and anticipation through variety. Experiment to discover what works best for your family. Use books, games, videos, props, made-up stories, songs, music or music videos, or even go on a family outing.

DO IT OFTEN!

We tend to find time for the things that are really important. It is best to set aside one evening per week (the same evening if possible) for family night. Remember, repetition is the best teacher. The more impressions you can create, the more of an impact you will make.

MAKE A MEMORY!

Find ways to make the lesson stick. For example, just as advertisers create "jingles" to help us remember their products, it is helpful to create family night "jingles" to remember the main theme—such as "It's best for you to seek what's true" or "Just like air, God is there!"

USE OTHER TOOLS FROM THE HERITAGE BUILDERS TOOL CHEST!

Family night is only one exciting way for you to intentionally build a loving heritage for your family. You'll also want to use these other exciting tools from Heritage Builders.

The Family Fragrance: There are five key qualities to a healthy family fragrance, each contributing to an environment of love in the home. It's easy to remember the Fragrance Five by fitting them into an acrostic using the word "Aroma"—

    A—Affection
    R—Respect
    O—Order
    M—Merriment
    A—Affirmation

Impression Points: Ways that we impress on our children our values, preferences, and concerns. We do it through our talk and our actions. We do it intentionally (through such methods as Family Nights), and we do it incidentally.

The Right Angle: The Right Angle is the standard of normal healthy living against which our children will be able to measure their atttitudes, actions, and beliefs.

Traditions: Meaningful activities which promote the process of passing on emotional, spiritual, and relational inheritance between generations. Family traditions can play a vital role in this process.

Please see the back of the book for information on how to receive the FREE Heritage Builders Newsletter which contains more information about these exciting tools! Also, look for the new book, *The Heritage,* available at your local Christian bookstore.

How to Use This Tool Chest

Summary page: For those who like the bottom line, we have provided a summary sheet at the start of each family night session. This abbreviated version of the topic briefly highlights the goal, key Scriptures, activity overview, main points, and life slogan. On the reverse side of this detachable page there is space provided for you to write down any ideas you wish to add or alter as you make the lesson your own.

Step-by-step: For those seeking suggestions and directions for each step in the family night process, we have provided a section which walks you through every activity, question, Scripture reading, and discussion point. Feel free to follow each step as written as you conduct the session, or read through this portion in preparation for your time together.

À la carte: We strongly encourage you to use the material in this book in an "à la carte" manner. In other words, pick and choose the questions, activities, Scriptures, age-appropriate ideas, etc. which best fit your family. This book is not intended to serve as a curriculum, requiring compliance with our sequence and plan, but rather as a tool chest from which you can grab what works for you and which can be altered to fit your family situation.

The long and the short of it: Each family night topic presented in this book includes several activities, related Scriptures, and possible discussion items. Do not feel it is necessary to conduct them all in a single family night. You may wish to spread one topic over several weeks using smaller portions of each chapter, depending upon the attention span of the kids and the energy level of the parents. Remember, short and effective is better than long and thorough.

Journaling: Finally, we have provided space with each session for you to capture a record of meaningful comments, funny happenings, and unplanned moments which will inevitably occur during family night. Keep a notebook of these journal entries for future reference. You will treasure this permanent record of the heritage passing process for years to come.

℮ Special Notes

1. Remove distractions. Start all activities sitting around a clean table even if you are only going to be there for a prayer before beginning an object lesson.

2. Do not force children to participate. If you have two or more children and one loses interest, then let that child come and go. He or she will usually stay in the area of the activity, and it is surprising how much kids learn even when you think they are not paying attention.

3. Use Christian videos to reinforce the stories used in Family Night activities. New videos make a great Family Night all by themselves. For example, the Veggie Tales movie, *The Fib from Outerspace,* is an excellent Family Night on lying.

4. The formal sets up the informal. Refer to your Family Night lesson throughout the week. You can refer to Family Night lessons for months and years. The lessons and memory phrases can become part of your family language.

5. Use Christian books and children's Bibles to reinforce the stories used in Family Night activities. Here are some to get you started:
   - *The Preschoolers Bible* by V. Gilbert Beers
   - *The Children's Discovery Bible*
   - *The Lion Storyteller Bible* by Bob Hartman
   - *Jesus' Story of the Lost Sheep* by Lois Rock
   - *Kingdom Parables* by Christopher Lane & Sharon Dahl
   - *Adam Raccoon—Parables for Kids* by Glen Keane

⊚ 1: Different Roads

Exploring what it means to follow the "narrow" road

Scripture
• Matthew 7:13

ACTIVITY OVERVIEW		
Activity	Summary	Pre-Session Prep
Activity 1: The Narrow Road	Discover how difficult it is to choose the narrow road in life.	You'll need a narrow board, two cinder blocks or other similar items, and a Bible.
Activity 2: What Do You Do?	Role play situations and learn what it means to do the right thing even when it's unpopular.	None.

Main Points:

—It's not always easy to do what Jesus wants us to do.

—Jesus wants us to do the right thing.

LIFE SLOGAN: "Choose today; the narrow way."

Make it your own
In the space provided below, outline the flow and add any additional ideas to guide you through the process of conducting this family night.

Prayer & Praise Items
In the space provided below, list any items you wish to pray about or give praise for during this family night session.

Journal
In the space provided below, capture a record of any fun or meaningful things which happened during this family night session.

Session Tip

We intentionally have provided more material than we would expect to be used in a single "Family Night" session. You know your family's unique interests and life circumstances best, so feel free to adapt this lesson to meet your family members' needs. Remember, short and simple is better than long and comprehensive.

WARM-UP

Open with Prayer: Begin by having a family member pray, asking God to help everyone in the family understand more about Him through this time. After prayer, review your last lesson by asking these questions:

- **What did we learn about in our last lesson?**
- **What was the Life Slogan?**
- **Have your actions changed because of what we learned? If so, how?** Encourage family members to give specific examples of how they've applied learning from the past week.

Share: Today we're going to learn that there are two paths in life: the wide and the narrow path. We're going to see why Jesus wants us to choose the narrow way.

ACTIVITY 1: The Narrow Road

Point: It's not always easy to do what Jesus wants us to do.

 Supplies: You'll need toy blocks, a narrow board, two cinder blocks or other similar items, and a Bible.

Activity: Using items such as toy blocks, mark off a wide, eight-foot long path across the floor in your meeting room or perhaps outside on the driveway if it's a nice day. Make sure the path is clear and easy to traverse. Next to this path, set up two cinder blocks about six feet apart and place on them an eight-foot 2X4. Make sure the 2X4 is centered on the blocks and secure (so it won't easily fall off the blocks).

Read aloud Matthew 7:13. Then **share: We're going to experience what it's like to walk the "narrow path" in life and how it compares to the wide path. Then we'll talk about what that means for our lives.**

? Have family members take turns walking down the wide path. Then ask:

- **What was it like to walk this path?** (It was easy; lots of us could do this at the same time.)

? Next, have family members attempt to cross the "balance beam" or narrow path. Walk along side children to make sure they don't fall and hurt themselves while crossing the board. It may take a few tries for children to cross the narrow path. If they can't complete the narrow path, hold them and help them walk without falling. Then consider these questions:

- **What was it like to cross the narrow path?** (It wasn't easy; I fell off; I needed help.)
- **How is trying to walk the narrow path like trying to obey?** (Sometimes it's not easy; sometimes we keep disobeying even though we know it's not right.)

Share: When we face a choice, Jesus wants us to follow Him—to follow the narrow path. As we found out, that's not as easy as the wide path. But just as I was here to help you, we can have help to make it on the narrow path. We get that help from the Holy Spirit, who guides us; from church, which teaches us; and from Christian friends, who encourage us.

ACTIVITY 2: What Do You Do?

Point: Jesus wants us to do the right thing.

 Supplies: None.

Activity: Share: Doing what's right isn't always easy. Sometimes people will make fun of us or tease us because we love Jesus. But Jesus wants us to make good choices even if other people make fun of our choices.

Explain that you're going to do some role plays that help family members understand what it means to do what is right. Assign roles to both children and parents and have fun as you try these situations:

- **A boy or girl in church is crying. Other kids are ignoring that child and playing happily. What do you do?**
- **A neighborhood friend wants you to go push someone off a swing. Everyone else thinks that would be funny. What do you do?**

- A box of candy is sitting on a table. You've been asked not to eat candy until after supper. Another child goes up and eats some candy and then offers you some. What do you do?
- Kids are calling another child mean names at preschool. You are the only one not calling that child names. He looks at you just as he's about to cry. What do you do?

You may come up with other ideas that would work for this role-play time. After the role plays, consider these questions:

- **Was it easy to know what to do in these situations? Why or why not?** (Yes, I knew what the right thing was; no, I knew what was right, but I didn't want to do it every time.)
- **Why does Jesus want us to do the right thing, even if others make fun of us?** (Because we don't see all the consequences of our actions but Jesus sees everything and knows what is best; because He knows what's best for us; because we can help people.)

Share: Sometimes it's not easy to do the right thing because of what others want us to do. But Jesus wants us to trust Him and make good choices so we can grow closer to Him and learn to follow His ways.

Have volunteers share other ways they can do the right thing even when others don't agree with them.

WRAP-UP

Gather everyone in a circle and have family members take turns answering this question: **What's one thing you've learned about God today?**

Next, tell kids you've got a new "Life Slogan" you'd like to share with them.

Life Slogan: Today's Life Slogan is this: "Choose today; the narrow way." Have family members repeat the slogan two or three times to

Age Adjustments

OLDER CHILDREN AND TEENAGERS understand the challenge of following Jesus when others tease them or make them feel uncomfortable. Use this activity to begin a discussion about peer pressure and how it affects their decisions. Help your older children feel confident enough in their faith to make good choices—even when those choices might risk injuring a friendship. Spend time listening to your children's struggles and helping them come up with practical solutions to specific situations. Then pray together for strength to do the right thing in all circumstances.

OPTIONAL AGE ADJUSTMENT: Have older children write a short story or real-life experience of following Jesus in a difficult situation. Collect this story and similar stories in a Family Christian Heritage Album.

help them learn it. Then encourage them to practice saying it during the week so they can talk about it at your next family night session.

Close in Prayer: Allow time for each family member to share prayer concerns and answers to prayer. Then close your time together with prayer for each concern. Thank God for listening to and caring about us.

Remember to record your prayer requests so you can refer to them in the future as you see God answering them.

@ 2: The Hidden Treasure

Exploring the Parable of the Hidden Treasure

Scripture
• Matthew 13:44-46

ACTIVITY OVERVIEW		
Activity	Summary	Pre-Session Prep
Activity 1: Which Is Worth More?	Compare the worth of various items.	You'll need several items from your child's world (stuffed toy, candy bar, toys, etc.).
Activity 2: The Treasure Hunt	Go on a treasure hunt to find candies.	You'll need Hershey's Kisses candies, note cards, and a Bible.

Main Points:

—God loves us and protects us.

—God strengthens us and protects us from Satan.

LIFE SLOGAN: "Whatever this world has in store; heaven has more."

Make it your own
In the space provided below, outline the flow and add any additional ideas to guide you through the process of conducting this family night.

Prayer & Praise Items
In the space provided below, list any items you wish to pray about or give praise for during this family night session.

Journal
In the space provided below, capture a record of any fun or meaningful things which happened during this family night session.

Session Tip

We intentionally have provided more material than we would expect to be used in a single "Family Night" session. You know your family's unique interests and life circumstances best, so feel free to adapt this lesson to meet your family members' needs. Remember, short and simple is better than long and comprehensive.

WARM-UP

Open with Prayer: Begin by having a family member pray, asking God to help everyone in the family understand more about Him through this time. After prayer, review your last lesson by asking these questions:

- **What did we learn about in our last lesson?**
- **What was the Life Slogan?**
- **Have your actions changed because of what we learned? If so, how?** Encourage family members to give specific examples of how they've applied learning from the past week.

Share: Today we're going to learn that life with God is more valuable than anything else in the world.

ACTIVITY 1: Which Is Worth More?

Point: Things that are important to us don't always cost a lot of money.

 Supplies: You'll need several items from your child's world (stuffed toy, candy bar, toys, etc.).

Activity: Have children bring a variety of items they value to this family night activity. You may wish to help them choose some items so they represent a variety of costs and values. For example, you might suggest: a stuffed animal; a "we love you" note from a lunch box; a candy bar; a favorite toy; family pictures; a favorite blanket; and so on.

Place two items at a time on a table in front of your children and ask them to pick out which one is worth more. If you have more than one child, you may discover a variety of responses for any two items as one child will value something greater than another. Repeat this activity until you've compared lots of different items.

? Consider these questions:
- **How did you determine which item was worth more?** (I know how much it cost; I guessed based on how big the item was; I didn't really know.)
- **Besides what it cost, what is another way to determine the value of an item?** (How much it means to you; how much you like it.)

Age Adjustments

OLDER CHILDREN AND TEENAGERS will enjoy the "Price Is Right" variation of this activity. For each item kids bring to the family night, write on a note card the approximate cost of that item. Then place the items on a table and shuffle the cards. Have older children and teenagers try to match the price cards with the correct items. You can then repeat the activity by having children put the items in order of their emotional or sentimental value, rather than monetary value.

Share: When we compared items, we thought mostly about how much they cost. Some of our treasures cost a lot of money. But others cost very little (such as photographs, a note from a friend or family member). Sometimes we think an item is more valuable because of what it *means* to us. In Activity 2 we're going to learn about the most valuable thing we could possibly have—a relationship with God.

ACTIVITY 2: The Treasure Hunt

Point: Being with God in heaven is worth more than anything else.

Supplies: You'll need Hershey's Kisses candies, note cards, and a Bible.

Activity: Before this activity, hide ten bags of candy around the house. In the first bag, place one candy; in the second, place two; and so on until the tenth bag is filled with 10 candies. Choose hiding places for each bag and make up a clue that will lead children to those places for each successively larger pile of candy. For example, you might hide one candy in the dryer and write a clue that states: When you're finished spinning around and getting clean, you go here to dry off. Kids may think of the bathroom, but will eventually figure out to look in the dryer. Number your clues so you know which one to give out next as children trade candy bags in for the clue that will lead to the next-larger bag of candy.

NOTE: If you have more than one child, hide two or more bags

of the same number of candies at each location—enough so each child will get one. Then have children take turns trying to figure out the clues.

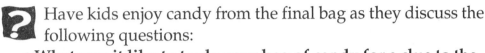 Explain to the children that they are going to go on a treasure hunt. Then give the first clue to your children and help as necessary until they find the bag with one candy. Tell them that there's a bag with more candy to be found too and that they can trade the single candy in for a clue that leads to that bag. Continue until children stop wanting to trade, or until they get to the last bag of candy. Then **read** aloud the story of the Hidden Treasure in Matthew 13:44-46.

Have kids enjoy candy from the final bag as they discuss the following questions:

- **What was it like to trade your bag of candy for a clue to the next larger bag?** (I wondered if there would be more candy in that bag; it was easy to trade for something better.)
- **How was our search for candy like the Bible story?** (We gave up something to get something better; we were searching for something of value.)
- **How did you feel as you found a bag with more candy?** (I felt good; I liked it; it was a good trade.)

Share: In the first game we played, we learned that some things of value cost a lot and some cost a little. In this game, we learned that it can be good to give up something of value for something with greater value. Our relationship with God is something of incredible value. If we love God, and trust Jesus as our Savior, we end up with the most valuable prize of all—eternal life with Jesus in heaven.

 Ask:
- **What kinds of things should we be willing to give up for God?** (Bad habits; toys we don't need; friends who aren't helping us grow toward God.)

Share: The world has lots of things that seem valuable, as we learned from our first activity. But a relationship with Jesus Christ is more valuable than all of them put together.

WRAP-UP
Gather everyone in a circle and have family members take turns answering this question: **What's one thing you've learned about God today?**

25

Next, tell kids you've got a new "Life Slogan" you'd like to share with them.

Life Slogan: Today's Life Slogan is this: "Whatever this world has in store; heaven has more." Have family members repeat the slogan two or three times to help them learn it. Then encourage them to practice saying it during the week so they can talk about it at your next family night session.

Close in Prayer: Allow time for each family member to share prayer concerns and answers to prayer. Then close your time together with prayer for each concern. Thank God for listening to and caring about us.

Remember to record your prayer requests so you can refer to them in the future as you see God answering them.

@ 3: The Fishing Net

Exploring how God decides who will go to heaven

Scripture
• Matthew 13:47-49
• John 3:16

ACTIVITY OVERVIEW		
Activity	Summary	Pre-Session Prep
Activity 1: Fishing Time	Build a fishing boat and net and act out the Bible story.	You'll need a large box, crayons or markers, a large bath towel, candy-size rocks, candy, wax paper, and a Bible.
Activity 2: More Good Fish	Choose a friend who they'll tell about Jesus and pray for.	You'll need some of the rocks from the first activity, plastic bags, paper, and pencils.

Main Points:

—God will separate those who believe in Jesus from those who don't.
—Share God's love with others so they can join us in heaven.

LIFE SLOGAN: "Believe so you will be; in God's net to see."

Make it your own
In the space provided below, outline the flow and add any additional ideas to guide you through the process of conducting this family night.

Prayer & Praise Items
In the space provided below, list any items you wish to pray about or give praise for during this family night session.

Journal
In the space provided below, capture a record of any fun or meaningful things which happened during this family night session.

We intentionally have provided more material than we would expect to be used in a single "Family Night" session. You know your family's unique interests and life circumstances best, so feel free to adapt this lesson to meet your family members' needs. Remember, short and simple is better than long and comprehensive.

WARM-UP

Open with Prayer: Begin by having a family member pray, asking God to help everyone in the family understand more about Him through this time. After prayer, review your last lesson by asking these questions:

- **What did we learn about in our last lesson?**
- **What was the Life Slogan?**
- **Have your actions changed because of what we learned? If so, how?** Encourage family members to give specific examples of how they've applied learning from the past week.

Share: Today we're going to learn how God chooses who gets into heaven and why it's important to tell our friends about God.

ACTIVITY 1: Fishing Time

Point: God will separate the good people from the bad people.

 Supplies: You'll need a large box, crayons or markers, a large bath towel, candy-size rocks, candy, wax paper, and a Bible.

Activity: To prepare for this activity, create a bunch of fake pieces of candy by rolling up candy-size rocks with wax paper or colored cellophane. You'll also need a supply of real candy wrapped to look somewhat similar.

Begin by having children help you build a fishing boat they can sit or stand in using a large cardboard box. Be creative and allow children to suggest ways to make the box look like a boat. Have plenty of fun decorating the boat, once it's taken shape.

When the boat is complete, give kids the bath towel or something else to be used as a net and explain that this will be their fish net. Have kids stand or sit in the boat and take turns tossing the net into the "lake" so it lands as flat as possible.

When they've had time to practice, **share: In Jesus' time, fishermen used nets to catch fish. They would sail out to where the fish were, lower their nets, and then scoop the fish up into the boat. What do you think it would be like to have lots of fish jumping around in your boat?**

Read aloud Matthew 13:47-49. Then have children get in their boat while you slide them across the floor as if sailing to a place where fish are jumping. Have kids toss out their net while you dump a mixture of candy and covered rocks onto the net. Have children carefully bring in the net to see what they caught. While still in the boat, have children separate the candy from the rocks and toss the rocks (carefully) back into the lake.

Age Adjustments

OLDER CHILDREN AND TEENAGERS may want to know more about this parable and how it applies to them. Often, when children near the teen years, they begin to doubt their faith or that they are Christians. Help them see that if they've accepted Christ as their Savior, they'll be taken to heaven when they die or when Jesus returns. Give them assurance of salvation, but also remind them that accepting Christ is the beginning of an ongoing, growing relationship that brings attitude and action changes.

Then drag the boat back to "shore" and have kids discuss the following questions while they enjoy their candy:
• **How is this activity like the story in the Bible?** (We went fishing.)
• **How is the way we separated the good candy from the rocks like the way God will separate those who believe from those who don't?**

Read John 3:16 to explain that those who believe in Jesus are like the candy and those who don't are like the rocks.

ACTIVITY 2: More Good Fish

Point: Share God's love with others so they can join us in heaven.

 Supplies: You'll need some of the rocks from the first activity, plastic bags, paper, and pencils.

Activity: Share: We've learned that God will someday separate the people who believe Him from those who don't. But how do people come to believe? (Others tell them; they read the Bible.)

Explain that one of the best ways for people to come to believe in Jesus is when others tell them about Him. Have kids share ways they can tell others about God's love. Then send kids back into their boat from the opening activity and drag them back to where the rocks are.

Have them each scoop up one or two rocks and take them back to the shore.

Have kids sit around a table with their rocks and think of someone they know that doesn't know Jesus. Have kids write the person's name on a slip of paper and put it into a plastic bag along with their rock. If kids don't know about their friend's faith commitment, that's okay. These rocks will be reminders for children to speak to their friends about God's love, and reminders for children to pray for their friends' salvation.

After each person has placed a rock and a slip of paper in a plastic bag, spend time in prayer, asking God to help you be bold in sharing your faith and to help "turn a few rocks into candy." Then **share: God wants us to tell others about Him. He wants the fishing nets to be full of people who will go to heaven one day, and we can help by sharing the good news with our friends. Let's keep these rocks as reminders to reach out to people who don't know Jesus, and to pray for them every day until they love God, and even after that so they can grow closer to God each day.**

Keep the rocks in a visible place in your house as a reminder of the importance of sharing God's love. If someone whose name is written on a slip of paper accepts Christ (or is found out to be a Christian already), celebrate together by removing that slip of paper and giving that person a piece of candy. Consider placing a new name in the bag. This activity helps children understand the importance of sharing faith, and of continually praying for others' salvation.

WRAP-UP

Gather everyone in a circle and have family members take turns answering this question: **What's one thing you've learned about God today?**

Next, tell kids you've got a new "Life Slogan" you'd like to share with them.

Life Slogan: Today's Life Slogan is this: "Believe so you will be; in God's net to see." Have family members repeat the slogan two or three times to help them learn it. Then encourage them to practice saying it during the week so they can talk about it at your next family night session.

Close in Prayer: Allow time for each family member to share prayer concerns and answers to prayer. Then close your time together with prayer for each concern. Thank God for listening to

and caring about us.

Remember to record your prayer requests so you can refer to them in the future as you see God answering them.

4: Jesus Walks on Water

Exploring what it means to keep your eyes focused on God

Scripture
• Matthew 14:22-32

ACTIVITY OVERVIEW		
Activity	Summary	Pre-Session Prep
Activity 1: Staying Focused	Look for a special penny, then look for a special gift.	You'll need one marked penny, lots of unmarked pennies, a wrapped gift for each child, and a Bible.
Activity 2: Looking Ahead	Attempt to walk a straight line without falling off.	You'll need masking tape.

Main Points:

—Don't be distracted by unimportant things.

—We must stay focused on Jesus so we don't fall.

LIFE SLOGAN: "Keep your eyes on Him; and you will not have to swim."

Make it your own

In the space provided below, outline the flow and add any additional ideas to guide you through the process of conducting this family night.

Prayer & Praise Items

In the space provided below, list any items you wish to pray about or give praise for during this family night session.

Journal

In the space provided below, capture a record of any fun or meaningful things which happened during this family night session.

Session Tip

We intentionally have provided more material than we would expect to be used in a single "Family Night" session. You know your family's unique interests and life circumstances best, so feel free to adapt this lesson to meet your family members' needs. Remember, short and simple is better than long and comprehensive.

WARM-UP

Open with Prayer: Begin by having a family member pray, asking God to help everyone in the family understand more about Him through this time. After prayer, review your last lesson by asking these questions:

- **What did we learn about in our last lesson?**
- **What was the Life Slogan?**
- **Have your actions changed because of what we learned? If so, how?** Encourage family members to give specific examples of how they've applied learning from the past week.

Share: Today we're going to learn about Peter's walk on water and why it's important to keep your eyes and heart focused on Jesus.

ACTIVITY 1: Staying Focused

Point: Don't be distracted by unimportant things.

 Supplies: You'll need one marked penny, lots of unmarked pennies, a wrapped gift for each child, and a Bible.

Activity: Hide a gift for each child somewhere in a particular room. Then, in that same room, toss a bunch of pennies onto the floor. Include one penny that has been marked by nail polish or a small piece of tape (make sure it is placed face-down on the floor).

Invite children into the room and tell them about the special penny. Then have them race to find the penny as soon as possible. If you have more than one child, you might want to consider hiding multiple marked pennies. Repeat this activity a number of times so each child has a chance to find the penny first.

 When children find the marked pennies, consider these questions:

- **While you were looking for the pennies, did you notice anything else in your room? Explain.** (No, I was focused on finding the penny; yes, I got distracted.)
- **Why was it important to stay focused on finding the penny?** (So we could do it quickly; so we wouldn't get distracted by other things; so we could win the game.)

Age Adjustments

OLDER CHILDREN AND TEENAGERS don't need a marked penny to play this game. Simply have older children seek for the oldest penny (make sure there is just one per child with this date).

Share: There is a gift of greater value somewhere in this room that you didn't see because you were looking for the marked pennies. See if you can find this gift now.

Make sure each child finds his or her gift and then have everyone form a circle to enjoy watching them open their gifts.

 Then consider these questions:

- **Did you notice the pennies while you were looking for your special gift? Why or why not?** (No, I just looked for the gift; no, I wanted to find the better prize.)
- **Why weren't you distracted by the pennies?** (Because we were looking for something greater; because we wanted the gift.)

Read Matthew 14:22-32 or summarize this story of Jesus walking on the water. Then **share: When you were looking for the marked pennies, you didn't notice other things in the room. But when you knew about a greater prize, you focused only on finding that prize. When we focus on something of importance, it's best not to be distracted by other things. In this story, Peter began to walk on the water because he focused on Jesus. But when he became distracted, he began to sink. We need to make sure we aren't distracted by unimportant things when we seek Jesus.**

ACTIVITY 2: Looking Ahead

Point: We must stay focused on Jesus so we don't fall.

 Supplies: You'll need masking tape.

Activity: Use masking tape to "draw" a line on the floor at least 10 feet long. Summarize the story of Jesus walking on the water again, then

share: We're going to see how important it is to stay focused on Jesus by trying a little experiment. One by one, we're going to take turns walking across this tape line—trying not to fall off the line.

? Choose your first line walker. Explain that he or she must look all around the room during the line-walking attempt. To encourage lots of distractions, have other family members attempt to get the walker's attention while he or she tries to walk on the line. Or make the line walker answer specific questions while he or she is trying to walk the line, such as: "When is your birthday? What day of the week is it? How old are you?" After each person has had a chance to walk while distracted, repeat the activity. This time, have one family member stand at the end of the masking-tape line and have the walker stay focused on that person throughout the entire attempt. Repeat for each family member. Then consider these questions:

- **How would Peter have done if he hadn't gotten distracted by the water or waves?** (He would have made it to Jesus; he wouldn't have fallen.)
- **How did it feel to walk the line when distracted?** (It wasn't easy; I kept falling off.)
- **How did it feel to walk the line when you focused on the person at the other end?** (It was easier; I didn't make as many mistakes.)
- **How is this like the way we should focus on Jesus in our daily walk?** (If we focus on Jesus, we'll make fewer mistakes; when we get distracted, we make bad choices.)

Share: When we get distracted from Jesus, we sometimes make bad choices. We need to keep our eyes on Jesus and trust Him because only our relationship with Jesus is eternal—everything else will someday be gone.

WRAP-UP

Gather everyone in a circle and have family members take turns answering this question: **What's one thing you've learned about God today?**

Next, tell kids you've got a new "Life Slogan" you'd like to share with them.

Age Adjustments

OLDER CHILDREN AND TEENAGERS who are struggling with materialism will be challenged by this lesson to consider what's really important in life. Help them to see that distractions from Jesus could include money, clothes, status with friends, and much more. Help your children see that focusing on God isn't an act of weakness, but a position of strength. Encourage them to place their trust in God—who will always be there for them—rather than material things.

Life Slogan: Today's Life Slogan is this: "Keep your eyes on Him; and you will not have to swim." Have family members repeat the slogan two or three times to help them learn it. Then encourage them to practice saying it during the week so they can talk about it at your next family night session.

Close in Prayer: Allow time for each family member to share prayer concerns and answers to prayer. Then close your time together with prayer for each concern. Thank God for listening to and caring about us.

Remember to record your prayer requests so you can refer to them in the future as you see God answering them.

⊚ 5: The Four Soils

Exploring the Parable of the Four Soils and what it means to hear and do the Word of God

Scripture
• Mark 4:3-8; 13-20

ACTIVITY OVERVIEW		
Activity	Summary	Pre-Session Prep
Activity 1: Four Corners	Create a "garden" that exemplifies the "four soils" in the parable.	You'll need a cake pan, aluminum foil, small stones, seeds, toothpicks, potting soil, a small flowerpot, and a Bible.
Activity 2: Roots	See how a plant without roots will blow away and learn the importance of growing "roots" in Christ.	You'll need a potted plant, lightweight cardboard, crayons, scissors, and a Bible.

Main Points:

—People, like plants, need good soil to grow.

—We must "root" ourselves in Jesus and live by God's Word.

LIFE SLOGAN: "Strong faith we keep; when roots grow deep."

Make it your own

In the space provided below, outline the flow and add any additional ideas to guide you through the process of conducting this family night.

Prayer & Praise Items

In the space provided below, list any items you wish to pray about or give praise for during this family night session.

Journal

In the space provided below, capture a record of any fun or meaningful things which happened during this family night session.

Session Tip

We intentionally have provided more material than we would expect to be used in a single "Family Night" session. You know your family's unique interests and life circumstances best, so feel free to adapt this lesson to meet your family members' needs. Remember, short and simple is better than long and comprehensive.

WARM-UP

Open with Prayer: Begin by having a family member pray, asking God to help everyone in the family understand more about Him through this time. After prayer, review your last lesson by asking these questions:

- **What did we learn about in our last lesson?**
- **What was the Life Slogan?**
- **Have your actions changed because of what we learned? If so, how?** Encourage family members to give specific examples of how they've applied learning from the past week.

Share: Today we're going to hear about seeds that fell in the ground, and how we need to grow roots in our relationship with Jesus.

ACTIVITY 1: Four Corners

Point: People, like plants, need good soil to grow.

 Supplies: You'll need a cake pan, aluminum foil, small stones, seeds, toothpicks, potting soil, a small flowerpot, and a Bible.

Activity: Have children sit around a table. Bring out a box the size of a cake pan (or a cake pan). Have kids help you line the box or pan with aluminum foil. Then give the following assignments for completing the box:

- Place small stones in one of the corners of the box.
- Fill a small flowerpot with potting soil and place it in another corner of the box.
- Place broken toothpicks in another corner of the box.
- Leave the fourth corner of the box bare.

Give children some seeds and have them "plant" the seeds in each of the four corners. In three of the corners, the seeds will be visible, but in the corner with the flowerpot, they should be buried underneath the soil.

When the seeds have been placed, **read** Mark 4:3-8 from the Bible or a Bible storybook, or summarize the story of the Four Soils in your own words. Have children point out which corners represents each of the soils from the story. (The stones represent the rocky places; the bare corner represents the path; the flowerpot represents the good soil; and the broken toothpicks represent the thorns.)

After reading or summarizing the story, consider these questions:
- **What happened to the seeds that landed on the path?** (Birds came and ate them.)
- **What happened to the seeds that fell on rocks?** (They were burned up by the sun.)
- **What happened to the seeds that were with the thorns?** (The thorns choked them and they died.)
- **What happened to the seeds that were sown on good soil?** (They grew and made more plants.)
- **Why did the seeds in the soil grow while the others didn't?** (Seeds need soil to grow; they were able to grow roots.)

Share: If we hear God's Word and plant it deep in our hearts, we will be like the seeds that were sown in the good soil. We will have a strong faith. But to grow, a plant needs more than soil— it needs water and sunshine. We too need things to grow in our faith with God.

Have family members share ways they can grow in their faith, such as: go to church; read the Bible; pray; talk with Christian friends; and so on.

Age Adjustments

OLDER CHILDREN AND TEENAGERS can be reminded daily of the need for growing in their relationship with God if they each plant a seed in a pot and care for it until it grows strong enough to be placed in a garden. Choose a sturdy flowering plant, such as a sunflower so your children can watch it turn from a small seed into a flowering giant. Have children water and care for their plants and be reminded daily that they need to grow their relationship with God in a similar, deliberate fashion.

ACTIVITY 2: Roots

Point: We must "root" ourselves in Jesus and live by God's Word.

 Supplies: You'll need a potted plant, lightweight cardboard, crayons, scissors, and a Bible.

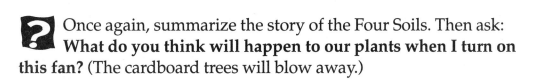

Activity: Have children each cut out and decorate a cardboard "tree." Help them to create a base for the tree so it can stand on its own. When the trees are completed, set them on a table next to a potted plant.

Set a fan a distance away from the table, pointed directly at the cardboard trees and potted plant.

Once again, summarize the story of the Four Soils. Then ask: **What do you think will happen to our plants when I turn on this fan?** (The cardboard trees will blow away.)

Turn on the fan and watch as the cardboard trees float away. Then consider these questions:
- **We learned in our previous activity that soil is needed for plants to grow. What does the seed do in the soil?** (Grow roots.)
- **Why didn't the plant in the pot blow away, like the cardboard trees?** (It has deep roots; it's stuck in the pot.)
- **How is the way this potted plant handled the wind like the way we should handle difficult situations?** (We need roots; we need to be solid in our faith.)

You may want to share about a time when the wind blew strong at your home and how the trees were able to survive if they had deep enough roots. Children may remember particularly strong windstorms.

Share: When a plant has deep and strong roots, it can stand up to the winds that blow. We can grow deep roots in our relationship with God by reading the Bible and learning from other Christians. That way, when we face a tough choice or a difficult situation, we can stay strong and do the right thing.

Have family members share how having strong faith roots can help them in everyday situations.

WRAP-UP
Gather everyone in a circle and have family members take turns answering this question: **What's one thing you've learned about God today?**

Next, tell kids you've got a new "Life Slogan" you'd like to share with them.

Life Slogan: Today's Life Slogan is this: "Strong faith we keep; when roots grow deep." Have family members repeat the slogan two or three times to help them learn it. Then encourage them to practice saying it during the week so they can talk about it at your next family night session.

Close in Prayer: Allow time for each family member to share prayer concerns and answers to prayer. Then close your time together with prayer for each concern. Thank God for listening to and caring about us.

Remember to record your prayer requests so you can refer to them in the future as you see God answering them.

☺ 6: Traveling Nativity

Exploring Jesus' birth

Scripture
• Luke 2
• Matthew 2

ACTIVITY OVERVIEW		
Activity	Summary	Pre-Session Prep
Activity 1: Nativity Set	Create a nativity set.	You'll need Styrofoam cones and balls of various sizes, a large box, markers or paints, and a Bible.
Activity 2: The Journey	Use the nativity characters to act out the Christmas story.	You'll need the items created in activity one, and a Bible.

Main Points:

—The Christmas story is about Jesus' birth.

—People came to see Jesus and bring Him gifts.

LIFE SLOGAN: "Kings, shepherds, and angels came to see; the baby Jesus, born to Joseph and Mary."

Make it your own
In the space provided below, outline the flow and add any additional ideas
to guide you through the process of conducting this family night.

Prayer & Praise Items
In the space provided below, list any items you wish to pray about or give
praise for during this family night session.

Journal
In the space provided below, capture a record of any fun or meaningful
things which happened during this family night session.

Session Tip

We intentionally have provided more material than we would expect to be used in a single "Family Night" session. You know your family's unique interests and life circumstances best, so feel free to adapt this lesson to meet your family members' needs. Remember, short and simple is better than long and comprehensive.

WARM-UP

Open with Prayer: Begin by having a family member pray, asking God to help everyone in the family understand more about Him through this time. After prayer, review your last lesson by asking these questions:

- **What did we learn about in our last lesson?**
- **What was the Life Slogan?**
- **Have your actions changed because of what we learned?**
  If so, how? Encourage family members to give specific examples of how they've applied learning from the past week.

Share: Today we're going to talk about Jesus' birth, and about the people who came to see Him.

ACTIVITY 1: Nativity Set

Point: The Christmas story is about Jesus' birth.

Supplies: You'll need Styrofoam cones and balls of various sizes, a large box, markers or paints, and a Bible.

Activity: Ask children what a "nativity set" is. If they don't know, explain that it's a collection of figures and animals that represent people who were at Jesus' birth or who came after He was born to worship Him.

Explain that you're going to create a unique nativity set. Have children paint and decorate Styrofoam cones and balls of various sizes so they look like people or animals in the Christmas story.

 Read or summarize the Christmas story for children from Luke 2 and Matthew 2, reminding them of the various characters

47

involved. Then have children help you list all the people and animals they'd like to have for their nativity set. This could include: Mary, Joseph, shepherds, kings or wise men, angels, baby Jesus, and various animals including sheep, cows, and camels.

When you've created all of your nativity characters, help children decorate a box placed on its side as the stable. Kids may also want to create a cardboard stable. This can be done by cutting two small holes in the bottom of a small rectangle of cardboard, then fitting that piece of cardboard on the tops of two small cone-shaped supports. Also, have kids create a star that can hang above the stable.

 When the nativity elements are complete, consider these questions:
- **What did you learn about the Christmas story as we worked on this nativity set?** (Lots of people came to see Jesus; the Christmas story is about Jesus' birth.)
- **What do we celebrate at Christmas?** (Jesus' birth; the story of Jesus.)

Age Adjustments

OLDER CHILDREN AND TEENAGERS may enjoy getting creative with their nativity set. Allow them to use such items as Lego building blocks, or other more creative supplies to build their scene. Have fun with the creation of the nativity and acknowledge your children's good ideas.

Share: The Christmas story has lots of characters, but all are focused on one thing—the birth of Jesus. In our next activity, we're going to relive the story of Jesus' birth and see how all of these characters relate to the Christmas story.

ACTIVITY 2: The Journey

Point: People came to see Jesus and bring Him gifts.

 Supplies: You'll need the items created in activity one, and a Bible.

Activity: Help children choose different rooms in your house (or different areas in one room) to represent the following locations: Nazareth; fields; the Far East; heaven; and Bethlehem.

Have children place the nativity set items in their proper "starting place" as listed below:
- Place the stable, manger, and animals in Bethlehem.
- Place Joseph and Mary in Nazareth.

- Place the shepherds in the fields.
- Place the kings or wise men in the Far East.
- Place the angels in heaven.

Explain that you're going to relive the Christmas story with your nativity set. Have children help you move the various characters around as you **read** or summarize the Christmas story. Make this a fun time of running around and "walking" the Styrofoam cone characters toward their goal—Bethlehem. Make sure Mary and Joseph get there first. Then place baby Jesus in the manger. After that, hang the star above the stable and place the angels around it. Next, have the shepherds and kings arrive and complete the scene.

You may want to consider starting this activity on the first Sunday of December, and then have the children move the various nativity characters closer to Bethlehem each week; culminating the scene Christmas Eve night.

> ## Age Adjustments
>
> OLDER CHILDREN AND TEENAGERS might enjoy videotaping their younger siblings as they reenact moving the nativity characters toward Bethlehem, the birth of baby Jesus, and the arrival of the shepherds and wisemen.

As you enact the scene, ask children to think about what each character might be thinking. For example, you might ask: What do you think Mary was thinking when she gave birth to Jesus? What do you think the shepherds were thinking as they traveled to Bethlehem? Why do you think the kings brought gifts?

When you've completed the nativity scene, talk about the celebration that took place in Bethlehem and in heaven and why people were so excited about the birth of this little baby.

Share: Jesus' birth was a wonderful event. All of heaven rejoiced when Jesus was born. People came bringing gifts for this baby who they believed was the Messiah—the person who would save them from sin. Indeed, Jesus did save them from sin when He died on the cross, and rose from the dead three days later. When we celebrate Christmas, we usually think of Christmas trees, gifts, and pretty decorations. Let us always remember the real meaning of Christmas when we look at our nativity set.

WRAP-UP

Gather everyone in a circle and have family members take turns answering this question: **What's one thing you've learned about God today?**

Next, tell kids you've got a new "Life Slogan" you'd like to share with them.

Life Slogan: Today's Life Slogan is this: "Kings, shepherds, and angels came to see; the baby Jesus, born to Joseph and Mary." Have family members repeat the slogan two or three times to help them learn it. Then encourage them to practice saying it during the week so they can talk about it at your next family night session.

 **Close in Prayer:** Allow time for each family member to share prayer concerns and answers to prayer. Then close your time together with prayer for each concern. Thank God for listening to and caring about us.

Remember to record your prayer requests so you can refer to them in the future as you see God answering them.

⊚ 7: The Good Samaritan

Exploring why it's important to put others' needs above our own

Scripture
• Luke 10:25-37

ACTIVITY OVERVIEW		
Activity	Summary	Pre-Session Prep
Activity 1: Lights, Camera, Action!	Act out the story of the Good Samaritan.	You'll need a children's storybook on the Good Samaritan, materials to make a "clacker" (see lesson), paper, markers, costumes, and a Bible.
Activity 2: A Candy Gift?	Decide what to do with candy they've been given.	You'll need candy.

Main Points:

—Love means putting others' needs above our own.
—God wants us to give to others in love.

LIFE SLOGAN: "Do what you should; to others be good."

Make it your own
In the space provided below, outline the flow and add any additional ideas to guide you through the process of conducting this family night.

Prayer & Praise Items
In the space provided below, list any items you wish to pray about or give praise for during this family night session.

Journal
In the space provided below, capture a record of any fun or meaningful things which happened during this family night session.

WARM-UP

Open with Prayer: Begin by having a family member pray, asking God to help everyone in the family understand more about Him through this time. After prayer, review your last lesson by asking these questions:

- **What did we learn about in our last lesson?**
- **What was the Life Slogan?**
- **Have your actions changed because of what we learned? If so, how?** Encourage family members to give specific examples of how they've applied learning from the past week.

Share: Today we're going to look at the story of the Good Samaritan and learn that love means caring for others above ourselves.

ACTIVITY 1: Lights, Camera, Action!

Point: Love means putting others' needs above our own.

 Supplies: You'll need a children's storybook on the Good Samaritan, materials to make a "clacker" (see lesson), paper, markers, costumes, and a Bible

Activity: Explain that you're going to make a "movie" of a familiar Bible story. Begin by having children help you make a "clacker" like those used in movies to set the scene. All you need is two strips of wood (a cut-apart yardstick or two wooden rulers work just fine), duct tape, and a sheet of cardboard. Tape one strip of wood to the top of the cardboard (they should be approximately the same length). Then use the tape to make a "hinge" connecting the other piece of wood to the piece that's taped to cardboard. You should be able to open and close the two pieces of wood and make a "clack" sound when they close.

53

See illustration. Have volunteers decorate one side of the clacker cardboard with the movie name, "The Good Samaritan."

Read the story of the Good Samaritan from a children's Bible, or summarize it from your own Bible (Luke 10:25-37). Then have children help you determine who will play the different parts (you could even enlist the help of a family pet, if you wish). You may wish to have kids come up with their own costumes too. Create a "scene paper" for each of the scenes your children decide to act out (which will be attached to the clacker at the beginning of a scene). Then have children act out the story. Start each scene by snapping the clacker and announcing, "Scene one, take one, action!" Encourage creativity and fun during this play-acting time.

When you've acted out the story, form a circle and consider the following questions:
- **Why did Jesus share this story?** (To remind us to take care of people; to let us know who is our neighbor.)
- **What did you learn from this story?** (We should care for those who are in need; everyone is our neighbor.)
- **What does this story show us about love?** (Love means helping people; love is more than a word.)

Share: Love means putting others' needs above our own. The Good Samaritan didn't think about his needs, but the needs of the person who was hurt. We too can look out for the needs of others.

ACTIVITY 2: A Candy Gift

Point: God wants us to give to others in love.

 Supplies: You'll need candy.

Activity: Have your children leave the room and come back in one at a time. Have each child take a turn sitting across from you at a table. Place three pieces of candy in front of the child and **say: This candy is for you, or for you and the person across the table from you.** Then say nothing else as each child determines whether to keep or give up

Age Adjustments

OLDER CHILDREN AND TEENAGERS may want to make more of a production out of your "movie." Give them the option of actually directing and video-taping the various scenes for this story. Not only will they enjoy the idea of making a movie, they'll also fell more investment in the story and what it means for their lives. You can watch the videotape many times after the story is done, too!

some of the candy. Vary who is sitting across from your child—it could be either parent or an older child.

 After each child has determined what to do with the candy, consider these questions:

- **What were you thinking as you looked at the candy?** (I wanted it all for myself; I wanted to share it.)
- **Is it easy to put others' needs and wants above your own? Why or why not?** (No, I like getting things; yes, I know it's the right thing to do.)

Share: You may have felt pressure to give some of the candy to the person across from you, but God doesn't want us to give because we feel pressured to give. He wants us to give to others out of love.

Have family members brainstorm ways they can give to people in need. For example, children might suggest raking leaves or shoveling snow for a neighbor who doesn't have any children to help with yard work. Or, your family may decide to collect clothes and toys to give to a local mission. Or, you may decide to save enough money to sponsor a child in a third-world country. Consider lots of options that can be done out of love, then choose as many as possible to follow through on.

Age Adjustments

OLDER CHILDREN AND TEENAGERS might have a more difficult time giving unselfishly. Usually, younger children will happily donate toys to people who have few or none. However, older children who feel the pressure to fit in or who are struggling with self-esteem, may look to their belongings as "anchors" in their life. Help them to realize that giving out of love builds a closer relationship with God, which in turn grows self-esteem and confidence that will go with them for a lifetime.

WRAP-UP

Gather everyone in a circle and have family members take turns answering this question: **What's one thing you've learned about God today?**

Next, tell kids you've got a new "Life Slogan" you'd like to share with them.

Life Slogan: Today's Life Slogan is this: "Do what you should; to others be good." Have family members repeat the slogan two or three times to help them learn it. Then encourage them to practice saying it during the week so they can talk about it at your next family night session.

Close in Prayer: Allow time for each family member to share prayer concerns and answers to prayer. Then close your time together with prayer for each concern. Thank God for listening to and caring about us.

Remember to record your prayer requests so you can refer to them in the future as you see God answering them.

⊚ 8: The Lost Sheep

Exploring the Parable of the Lost Sheep

Scripture
• Luke 15:1-7

ACTIVITY OVERVIEW		
Activity	**Summary**	**Pre-Session Prep**
Activity 1: Sheep-in-a-Box	Learn about the lost sheep by watching the story portrayed with craft supplies.	You'll need a shoe box, felt, and pom pom balls.
Activity 2: Lost and Found	Act out what it must be like to be found by a shepherd.	You'll need a Bible and blindfolds.

Main Points:

— When a sheep is lost, the shepherd finds it.

— Jesus comes to find us when we are lost.

LIFE SLOGAN: "Jesus our Shepherd comes around; until the lost are found."

Make it your own
In the space provided below, outline the flow and add any additional ideas
to guide you through the process of conducting this family night.

Prayer & Praise Items
In the space provided below, list any items you wish to pray about or give
praise for during this family night session.

Journal
In the space provided below, capture a record of any fun or meaningful
things which happened during this family night session.

Session Tip

We intentionally have provided more material than we would expect to be used in a single "Family Night" session. You know your family's unique interests and life circumstances best, so feel free to adapt this lesson to meet your family members' needs. Remember, short and simple is better than long and comprehensive.

WARM-UP

Open with Prayer: Begin by having a family member pray, asking God to help everyone in the family understand more about Him through this time. After prayer, review your last lesson by asking these questions:

- **What did we learn about in our last lesson?**
- **What was the Life Slogan?**
- **Have your actions changed because of what we learned? If so, how?** Encourage family members to give specific examples of how they've applied learning from the past week.

Share: Today we're going to learn about how shepherds take care of their sheep, and how Jesus cares for us in the same way.

ACTIVITY 1: Sheep-in-a-Box

Point: When a sheep is lost, the shepherd finds it.

Supplies: You'll need a shoe box, felt, and pom pom balls.

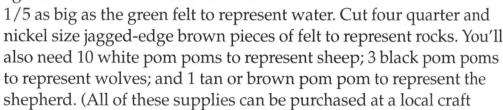

Activity: Before the family night activity, designate a shoebox to hold the "story-in-a-box" materials. Cut a large salad-plate-size piece of green felt to represent "grass." Cut a blue oval of felt about 1/5 as big as the green felt to represent water. Cut four quarter and nickel size jagged-edge brown pieces of felt to represent rocks. You'll also need 10 white pom poms to represent sheep; 3 black pom poms to represent wolves; and 1 tan or brown pom pom to represent the shepherd. (All of these supplies can be purchased at a local craft store.) Place all of these items in a box.

Young children love the curiosity and anticipation that comes with opening and taking things out of a box. Follow these instructions to use the items for telling the story of the lost sheep.

1. Open the box slowly and pull out the green felt. Ask children what they think it might represent. After they guess, explain that it is the grass.

2. Pull out the blue felt and once again ask what it might be. Explain that it is water and then place it on the green felt, near one edge.

3. Remove the brown felt pieces, ask what they might be, then place them on the other side of the felt, away from the water, explaining that they represent rocks.

4. Place the 10 white pom poms next to the water. **Say: Ten sheep were getting drinks near the water. Can you count them?** (Help children count the sheep.) **How do you think the sheep felt as they stood together near the water?**

5. Place the three black pom poms near the rocks. Explain that these pom poms represent wolves. Slowly move one of the sheep toward the rocks and **say: One of the sheep wandered away and got lost. How do you think this lost sheep feels as he realizes he's surrounded by wolves?**

6. Move the tan or brown pom pom to the rocks, explaining that it is the shepherd. **Say: The shepherd came to count his 10 sheep. Let's count them again.** (Count the 9 remaining sheep.) **Oh dear! One sheep is missing. What do you think the shepherd will do?**

7. Move the shepherd to the rocks to find the lost sheep. **Say: The shepherd is very happy when he finds the lost sheep and he carries it back to the water where the other sheep are waiting.** Place the lost sheep pom pom on the shepherd pom pom and move them both back to the water. **Ask: How does the lost sheep feel now that it's back with the group?**

Share: When a shepherd notices a sheep is missing, he goes looking for that sheep. The shepherd doesn't want to lose even 1 sheep. Even if he had 100 sheep, he would look for the lost sheep. In the same way, Jesus is our Shepherd and comes to find us if we stray or go down a wrong path. He wants to help us avoid the wolves that may come our way.

Age Adjustments

OLDER CHILDREN may prefer to act out the story of the lost sheep—especially the part where the wolves are hungrily eyeing the lost sheep! Give them the option of acting out this story in a fun way. Have one person play the part of the lost sheep, another, the part of the wolf (representing lots of wolves) and another, the shepherd. Afterward, discuss how family members felt in their role and how that compare to the way we feel about Jesus as our Shepherd.

ACTIVITY 2: Lost and Found

Point: Jesus comes to find us when we are lost.

 Supplies: You'll need a Bible and blindfolds.

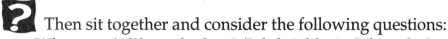

Activity: Read aloud Luke 15:1-7 or summarize the story for children.
Then **share: Jesus is our Shepherd and doesn't want us to wander away from Him. What are some ways we might wander away in life?** Share some examples, such as: lie, cheat, skip church, do something mean to another person.

Then explain that you're going to help children see how much Jesus cares for us. Have family members take turns wearing a blindfold, and wandering around the house, as if lost. After allowing time for that person to get "lost," send someone along to guide him or her back to your meeting room. Repeat this game so each family member gets a chance to be lost and to be the "finder."

Then sit together and consider the following questions:
- **What was it like to be lost?** (I didn't like it; I thought I might run into something.)
- **What was it like to be found by another family member?** (I felt safe; I didn't worry about bumping into things anymore.)
- **How did it feel to be the "finder" in this game?** (I liked helping someone; I worried about the lost person getting hurt.)

Share: When someone wanders away from Jesus, we worry about that person. But Jesus seeks that person out to remind him how much He loves him. We too can help each other by sharing God's love when someone wanders away from God. Let's pray for God to give us wisdom to know what to say to people who stray; and to make good choices so we don't stray far from Jesus.

Optional Activity: Play a version of pin the tail on the donkey called "Pin the Staff on the Sheep." Attach a construction paper cutout of a sheep (perhaps a "creation" of one of the children) onto a safe vertical surface. Then blindfold each child "shepherd" and have him or her "find the sheep" by sticking a Scotch-taped paper staff

onto it. If the child misses, the sheep is still lost.

Close with prayer.

WRAP-UP

Gather everyone in a circle and have family members take turns answering this question: **What's one thing you've learned about God today?**

Next, tell kids you've got a new "Life Slogan" you'd like to share with them.

Life Slogan: Today's Life Slogan is this: "Jesus our Shepherd comes around; until the lost are found." Have family members repeat the slogan two or three times to help them learn it. Then encourage them to practice saying it during the week so they can talk about it at your next family night session.

Close in Prayer: Allow time for each family member to share prayer concerns and answers to prayer. Then close your time together with prayer for each concern. Thank God for listening to and caring about us.

Remember to record your prayer requests so you can refer to them in the future as you see God answering them.

⊚ 9:Lazarus

Exploring how God gave Jesus power over death

Scripture
• John 11

ACTIVITY OVERVIEW		
Activity	Summary	Pre-Session Prep
Activity 1: A Sad Day	Talk about sad things and learn that Jesus was sad when Lazarus died.	You'll need a children's Bible storybook or a Bible or the children's video, *The Easter Promise.*
Activity 2: Unwrapped	Act out the story of Lazarus.	You'll need toilet paper rolls.

Main Points:

—Jesus cried just like we do.

—Jesus has power over death.

LIFE SLOGAN: "To God Jesus talked; and out Lazarus walked."

Make it your own

In the space provided below, outline the flow and add any additional ideas to guide you through the process of conducting this family night.

Prayer & Praise Items

In the space provided below, list any items you wish to pray about or give praise for during this family night session.

Journal

In the space provided below, capture a record of any fun or meaningful things which happened during this family night session.

We intentionally have provided more material than we would expect to be used in a single "Family Night" session. You know your family's unique interests and life circumstances best, so feel free to adapt this lesson to meet your family members' needs. Remember, short and simple is better than long and comprehensive.

WARM-UP

Open with Prayer: Begin by having a family member pray, asking God to help everyone in the family understand more about Him through this time. After prayer, review your last lesson by asking these questions:

- **What did we learn about in our last lesson?**
- **What was the Life Slogan?**
- **Have your actions changed because of what we learned? If so, how?** Encourage family members to give specific examples of how they've applied learning from the past week.

Share: Today we're going to talk about a man named Lazarus, and how Jesus brought him back from the dead.

ACTIVITY 1: A Sad Day

Point: Jesus cried just like we do.

 Supplies: You'll need a children's Bible storybook or a Bible or the children's video, *The Easter Promise.*

Activity: Open the family night by asking kids to share things that make them feel sad. You might begin by sharing one of your own "sad stories." Be sensitive to children who may have just lost a friend, pet, or even a toy they really liked. Help them to know that it's okay to feel sad about things.

Then tell children that even Jesus was sad at times. Share the story of Lazarus from John 11, using your own words, reading from a children's Bible storybook, or showing the video, *The Easter Promise* (Christian Broadcasting Network, 1996). Be sure to include the following points in your story:

- Lazarus was Jesus' friend.
- Lazarus was sick, then he died.

Heritage
BUILDERS

- Lazarus' sisters said to Jesus, "If You had been here, my brother wouldn't have died."
- Jesus cried for his friend Lazarus.
- Jesus prayed and thanked God for hearing Him.
- Lazarus came out with strips of linen wrapped on his hands, feet, and face.

 Consider these questions:

- **Were you surprised when Jesus was sad? Explain.** (Yes, I thought He would always be happy; no, Jesus could cry just like me.)

- **Why are we sometimes sad?** (Because someone did something mean to us; because we did something wrong.)

Share: When something bad happens to us or to someone we love, we feel sad. Jesus understands what it feels like to be sad, because He was sad too. When we're sad, we can ask Jesus to comfort us and bring us joy again.

Age Adjustments

OLDER CHILDREN AND TEENAGERS will be able to go deeper with this discussion. Help them to see what it means that Jesus experienced the same emotions they've experienced. Ask your children: "How does knowing Jesus felt sadness help you when you feel sad?" and "What other emotions do you think Jesus felt?"

ACTIVITY 2: Unwrapped

Point: Jesus has power over death.

 Supplies: You'll need toilet paper rolls.

Activity: Explain that when people died in Jesus' day, they were wrapped in cloths and placed in a tomb.

Ask a child to pretend he or she is Lazarus. Then help the rest of your family members wrap that child in toilet paper, beginning with the feet and continuing until the child is wrapped from head to toe. Even older siblings and Mom and Dad might enjoy being wrapped up in this way.

When your Lazarus is ready, help him or her to lie down on the floor. Then act out the story using the following simple dialogue (or something similar):

Mary: Jesus, if You had been here, my brother Lazarus would not have died.

Jesus: (Praying) Father, thank You for hearing My prayer. (Holding arms out to the side) Lazarus, get up!

Lazarus can then break out of the toilet paper and jump up joyfully. Have everyone join together in a group hug.

 Consider these questions:
- **Why was Jesus sad when He heard about Lazarus?** (Lazarus was His friend; He loved Lazarus.)
- **Why could Jesus raise Lazarus from the dead?** (Because He had God's power; because He prayed for God to raise him.)
- **What do we learn about Jesus from this story?** (Jesus felt sad like we do sometimes; Jesus has lots of power.)

WRAP-UP

Gather everyone in a circle and have family members take turns answering this question: **What's one thing you've learned about God today?**

Next, tell kids you've got a new "Life Slogan" you'd like to share with them.

Life Slogan: Today's Life Slogan is this: "To God Jesus talked; and out Lazarus walked." Have family members repeat the slogan two or three times to help them learn it. Then encourage them to practice saying it during the week so they can talk about it at your next family night session.

Close in Prayer: Allow time for each family member to share prayer concerns and answers to prayer. Then close your time together with prayer for each concern. Thank God for listening to and caring about us.

Remember to record your prayer requests so you can refer to them in the future as you see God answering them.

@ 10: Dorcas—Helping Others

Exploring the value of doing good things and helping others

Scripture
- 1 Corinthians 13:4
- Acts 9:36-42

ACTIVITY OVERVIEW		
Activity	Summary	Pre-Session Prep
Activity 1: Making Clothes	Make and decorate "shirts" for one another.	You'll need large pillow-cases, fabric markers, scissors, and a Bible.
Activity 2: Clothes for Others	Collect (and purchase) clothes and deliver them to a needy family or mission.	You'll need newsprint or a large sheet of paper, markers or crayons, children's clothing, money to purchase a new clothing item, and a Bible.

Main Points:

—Dorcas made clothes and did good things.

—We can do good things for others.

LIFE SLOGAN: "Help those with needs; by doing good deeds."

Make it your own
In the space provided below, outline the flow and add any additional ideas to guide you through the process of conducting this family night.

Prayer & Praise Items
In the space provided below, list any items you wish to pray about or give praise for during this family night session.

Journal
In the space provided below, capture a record of any fun or meaningful things which happened during this family night session.

WARM-UP

Open with Prayer: Begin by having a family member pray, asking God to help everyone in the family understand more about Him through this time. After prayer, review your last lesson by asking these questions:

- **What did we learn about in our last lesson?**
- **What was the Life Slogan?**
- **Have your actions changed because of what we learned? If so, how?** Encourage family members to give specific examples of how they've applied learning from the past week.

Share: Today we're going to learn about a woman named Dorcas, who was always doing good things for others.

ACTIVITY 1: Making Clothes

Point: Dorcas made clothes and did good things.

Supplies: You'll need large pillowcases, fabric markers, scissors, and a Bible.

Activity: Begin by telling family members about Dorcas, a woman who loved to make clothing and help others. Then explain that you're all going to make clothing too. Help children cut head and arm holes in the large pillow cases to make night shirts or play shirts. Have kids try on the shirts to make sure they fit. Enjoy this time together—it's okay to laugh if the clothing looks funny.

Then have children use the fabric paints or markers to decorate their shirts with images or words that suggest "helping others." **Share** the story of Dorcas from Acts 9:36-42 as children decorate their shirts.

After the shirts are done, have family members model them for each other. Then consider these questions:

- **What was it like to make our own shirts?** (It was fun; it was hard.)
- **How would you feel if someone we knew made clothes for us?** (That would be cool; I would like that; I would tell that person thanks.)

Age Adjustments

OLDER CHILDREN AND TEENAGERS have the skills necessary to actually sew their own shirts. While this will take more time and effort, the resulting lesson will be worth it. Help older children learn how to use a pattern, cloth, and a sewing machine (or hand-stitching) to create a simple T-shirt for themselves. As you help children through the frustrations that inevitably occur, you can help them see what a great service Dorcas was providing for others. Your children will respect Dorcas' unselfishness and begin to grasp the value of helping others.

Have children tell about friends or relatives who have done nice things for them. For example, someone might talk about a grandparent who took him to the zoo; or about a friend who shared a candy bar at school.

Share: Dorcas had been a great helper to many people. She was well known for all the great clothes she made for others. But one day, she became sick and soon died. God gave Peter the power to bring Dorcas back from the dead so she could continue helping others and doing good things.

Have family members tell about good things they've done for others. Then celebrate together how each member of your family has been a good helper—just like Dorcas.

ACTIVITY 2: Clothes for Others

Point: We can do good things for others.

 Supplies: You'll need newsprint or a large sheet of paper, markers or crayons, children's clothing, money to purchase a new clothing item, and a Bible.

Activity: Place a sheet of newsprint or large paper on a table (or tape it to a wall). Have children brainstorm ways people can help others (such as doing yard work, making clothes, providing meals, baby-sitting children, and so on). Have kids list as many items as possible on this paper—filling it up if at all possible.

 When the list is complete, consider these questions:

- **What does this list tell us about helping people?** (There are lots of ways to help people; people have lots of needs.)

- **Why does the Bible teach us to help others?** (Because that's what Jesus would do; because it's good to help.)
- **Which of the things on our list can we do to help others?** (Have someone circle all those your family can do.)
- **Which of these things would you like to do to help others?** (Answers will vary.)

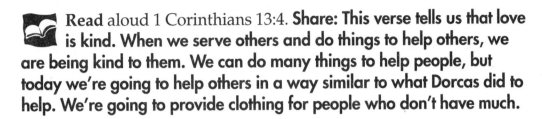 **Read** aloud 1 Corinthians 13:4. **Share: This verse tells us that love is kind. When we serve others and do things to help others, we are being kind to them. We can do many things to help people, but today we're going to help others in a way similar to what Dorcas did to help. We're going to provide clothing for people who don't have much.**

With your children's help, go through clothing drawers and collect as much good-quality clothing as you can that you can donate to a local mission. As each family member places an item of clothing in a bag or box, have that person say, "I want to be a helping hand." When you've collected all the items, let your family members know you're also going to shop for a new item of clothing to include in the box. If children would like to contribute to the purchase of the item, that's fine, but don't force them.

Go together to a store and have children help you find a nice shirt, dress, or other clothing item that a child might enjoy. Buy that item and include it with your delivery to the local mission.

Another option is to have a neighborhood garage sale to sell used clothes and toys, then take the money to buy new clothing items for the mission.

After delivering the clothing, consider these questions:
- **What was it like to give up your clothes for others?** (I'm glad I'm helping someone; it wasn't easy, because I liked that shirt.)
- **How is what we did like what Dorcas** (and many other Bible characters) **did?** (We helped people; we gave someone clothing.)

Share: God smiles on us when we help others. And besides, it feels good to do things for others!

WRAP-UP

Gather everyone in a circle and have family members take turns answering this question: **What's one thing you've learned about God today?**

Next, tell kids you've got a new "Life Slogan" you'd like to share with them.

Life Slogan: Today's Life Slogan is this: "Help those with needs; by doing good deeds." Have family members repeat the slogan two or three times to help them learn it. Then encourage them to practice saying it during the week so they can talk about it at your next family night session.

Close in Prayer: Allow time for each family member to share prayer concerns and answers to prayer. Then close your time together with prayer for each concern. Thank God for listening to and caring about us.

Remember to record your prayer requests so you can refer to them in the future as you see God answering them.

@ 11: Priscilla—Hospitality

Exploring the story of Priscilla and her gift of hospitality

Scripture
• Acts 18:1-4, 18-26; Romans 16:3-5

ACTIVITY OVERVIEW		
Activity	Summary	Pre-Session Prep
Activity 1: Tent Meeting	Build a tent and learn how Priscilla and Aquila served Paul when he visited them.	You'll need a large sheet, a rope, clothespins, and a Bible.
Activity 2: Hosting a Meal	Learn about how to be hospitable and then prepare a meal for others to enjoy.	You'll need snacks and supplies for a nice meal.

Main Points:

—Priscilla had the gift of hospitality.

—People who have the gift of hospitality open their homes and serve others.

LIFE SLOGAN: "Hospitality is a gift; it gives others a lift.

Make it your own
In the space provided below, outline the flow and add any additional ideas to guide you through the process of conducting this family night.

Prayer & Praise Items
In the space provided below, list any items you wish to pray about or give praise for during this family night session.

Journal
In the space provided below, capture a record of any fun or meaningful things which happened during this family night session.

Session Tip

We intentionally have provided more material than we would expect to be used in a single "Family Night" session. You know your family's unique interests and life circumstances best, so feel free to adapt this lesson to meet your family members' needs. Remember, short and simple is better than long and comprehensive.

WARM-UP

Open with Prayer: Begin by having a family member pray, asking God to help everyone in the family understand more about Him through this time. After prayer, review your last lesson by asking these questions:

- **What did we learn about in our last lesson?**
- **What was the Life Slogan?**
- **Have your actions changed because of what we learned? If so, how?** Encourage family members to give specific examples of how they've applied learning from the past week.

Share: Today we're going to learn about Priscilla and her spiritual gift of hospitality.

ACTIVITY 1: Tent Meeting

Point: Priscilla had the gift of hospitality.

Supplies: You'll need a large sheet, a rope, clothespins, and a Bible.

Activity: Tell family members that you're going to become "tent-makers" just like Paul, Priscilla, and her husband Aquila, whose story is recorded in the New Testament. Find a place in your home where you can tie a rope taut about four feet above the ground. You could use a heavy 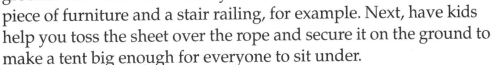 piece of furniture and a stair railing, for example. Next, have kids help you toss the sheet over the rope and secure it on the ground to make a tent big enough for everyone to sit under.

NOTE: If the weather is nice, you could do this outside (perhaps even using a clothesline). You may also consider putting up a camping tent.

Remain under this tent for the rest of this activity. Summarize the role that Priscilla played in Paul's life. Here are some points to make as you tell this story (from Acts 18:1-4, 18-26; Romans 16:3-5):

- Paul was a traveling missionary who was also a tentmaker.
- Paul needed a place to stay when he visited Corinth.
- Priscilla and her husband, Aquila, opened up their home to Paul—they were also tentmakers.
- All of them loved Jesus.
- When Paul stayed with Priscilla and her husband, he helped them make tents when he wasn't preaching.
- When Paul moved away from Corinth, Priscilla and her husband went with him to Ephesus.
- Once again, Priscilla and Aquila provided a place for Paul to stay in Ephesus.
- After Paul moved again, another preacher, Apollos, came and stayed with Priscilla.
- Priscilla and Aquila started a church in their home.

Then discuss these questions:
- **How did Priscilla help Paul and Apollos?** (She offered her home; she gave them a place to stay.)
- **What would it be like if we opened up our homes to people who were needing a place to say?** (I might have to give up my room; it would be fun.)

Age Adjustments

OLDER CHILDREN who sometimes have friends stay overnight will be able to grasp the concept of hospitality by reviewing their own experiences. Help them to see how their offer to a friend of a place to sleep and your offer of a meal or two is like what Priscilla did for Paul and other Christian brothers and sisters. Use this real-life example to help older children discover that hospitality is a gift of serving others.

Share: When you open up your home, cook meals, or otherwise serve others who have needs, you are being hospitable. Priscilla had the gift of hospitality. She opened up her home, served those who came, and probably fixed quite a few meals for Paul and others who were hungry. We too can be hospitable toward others.

ACTIVITY 2: Hosting a Meal

Point: People who have the gift of hospitality open their homes and serve others.

 Supplies: You'll need snacks and supplies for a nice meal.

Activity: Explain to children that hospitality is "making people feel at home" when they're at your house. Return to your tent with a snack and drink to serve one another. Enjoy a little "tea time" play and talk about how you've been made to feel at home at others' houses. You can add more fun to the activity by assigning character roles.

Whoever is serving is Priscilla, and each child gets a turn to be Priscilla while the other family members play Paul, Aquila, etc.

Consider these questions:
- **What does it feel like when you're at someone else's house and they give you a snack?** (It makes me feel good; I like it; I feel cared for.)
- **How have you made others feel at home at our house?** (I let them play with my toys; I get them something to drink; we've made supper for them.)

Have family members decide on another family they'd like to invite over for a meal. Call that family right away (from under the tent, if possible!) and set up a time for them to visit your home. (If you're uncomfortable serving a meal, you can consider ordering pizza and having a game night with this family.)

When the time comes for your meal, have family members each help in some way to present an enjoyable experience. Have younger kids help set the table and older children help to prepare the meal. Include time for conversation and game-playing if appropriate. Enjoy your time together, then debrief with the following questions after your guests leave or the next day:
- **What was it like to serve others?** (It was fun; I enjoyed it; it was hard work.)
- **How is what we did like what Priscilla did?** (We served others; we were good hosts.)

Share: Priscilla had the spiritual gift of hospitality. When she became a Christian, the Holy Spirit gave her that gift. There are many spiritual gifts—and every Christian has at least one. You might have the gift of wisdom, or of teaching, or of serving. But while we may not have the gift of hospitality as Priscilla did, we are called to serve one another with gladness.

Ask: What are gifts preschoolers might have? (Singing Scripture songs; helping others; giving.)

WRAP-UP

Gather everyone in a circle and have family members take turns answering this question: **What's one thing you've learned about God today?**

Next, tell kids you've got a new "Life Slogan" you'd like to share with them.

Life Slogan: Today's Life Slogan is this: "Hospitality is a gift; it gives others a lift." Have family members repeat the slogan two or three times to help them learn it. Then encourage them to practice saying it during the week so they can talk about it at your next family night session.

Close in Prayer: Allow time for each family member to share prayer concerns and answers to prayer. Then close your time together with prayer for each concern. Thank God for listening to and caring about us.

Remember to record your prayer requests so you can refer to them in the future as you see God answering them.

⊚ 12: Reflecting God's Love

Exploring what it means to hear God and reflect His love to others

Scripture
• James 1:19-25

ACTIVITY OVERVIEW		
Activity	Summary	Pre-Session Prep
Activity 1: Dress-up Time	Blindfold children and dress them up with one or more item of clothing out of place.	You'll need clothing, a large mirror, and a Bible.
Activity 2: Reflections	Shine a flashlight on objects and learn how we can reflect God's Word.	You'll need a Bible, a hand mirror, cardboard, and a flashlight.

Main Points:

—When we see something wrong with the way we act, we should fix it.

—God wants us to reflect His Word.

LIFE SLOGAN: "We must hear and obey so; others may see and know."

Make it your own
In the space provided below, outline the flow and add any additional ideas to guide you through the process of conducting this family night.

Prayer & Praise Items
In the space provided below, list any items you wish to pray about or give praise for during this family night session.

Journal
In the space provided below, capture a record of any fun or meaningful things which happened during this family night session.

Session Tip

We intentionally have provided more material than we would expect to be used in a single "Family Night" session. You know your family's unique interests and life circumstances best, so feel free to adapt this lesson to meet your family members' needs. Remember, short and simple is better than long and comprehensive.

WARM-UP

Open with Prayer: Begin by having a family member pray, asking God to help everyone in the family understand more about Him through this time. After prayer, review your last lesson by asking these questions:

- **What did we learn about in our last lesson?**
- **What was the Life Slogan?**
- **Have your actions changed because of what we learned? If so, how?** Encourage family members to give specific examples of how they've applied learning from the past week.

Share: Today we're going to learn what it means to reflect God's Word.

ACTIVITY 1: Dress-up Time

Point: When we see something wrong with the way we act, we should fix it.

Supplies: You'll need clothing, a large mirror, and a Bible.

Activity: Tell children you're going to play a dress-up game. Blindfold a child and then place some items of clothing on them, making sure to put at least one item on in a funny way. For example, you might place a sweater on inside-out; a scarf tied around the waist; or a belt wrapped around one leg. Lead the child to a large mirror and see how long it takes them to discover what item of clothing is out of place. Repeat this activity with all children at least a few times, making sub-tle changes for older children to discover and more obvious ones for younger children. Another way to "play" is to have the kids who aren't dressed silly sit at angles in front of the mirror and point out all the out-of-place clothing on the blindfolded child who is standing behind them (sort of a "What's Wrong with This Picture?" game).

 Then **ask:**

- **What did you notice each time you looked in the mirror?** (Something was out of place; there was something wrong about my clothes.)
- **How did you know something was out of place?** (I know how things are supposed to be; it looked funny.)

Read aloud or summarize James 1:22-24. Then consider these questions:

- **What does this story tell us?** (We should notice things that are wrong in our lives; it's not good to ignore things we're doing wrong.)
- **What are we supposed to do when we see something that's not right in our lives?** (We should change it; we should ask God what is right; we should do what God wants.)
- **How do we know when something is out of place in our lives?** (It doesn't seem right; it goes against the Bible; parents tell us.)

Share: We learn how to wear our clothes by watching our parents or our friends. We learn to live our lives by reading the Bible and listening to God's words. Just as we can tell when something is wrong in our clothing, we can tell when something doesn't match what Jesus would want us to do. When we see something that doesn't fit right, we need to listen to God, and do what He says. We need to fix the things that are wrong.

Age Adjustments

Help OLDER CHILDREN AND TEENAGERS discover the importance of "holding up a mirror" to their actions by reviewing some decisions they've made in the last few months. Don't use this time to rehash the mistakes, however. Instead, help them to see what they could have done differently in certain instances. Be sure to include an example from your life as well, so it doesn't feel like you're punishing them all over again. Take time to learn from your mistakes and discover how to hold up that mirror to see what's right and what's wrong in behaviors and actions.

ACTIVITY 2: Reflections

Point: God wants us to reflect His Word.

 Supplies: You'll need a Bible, a hand mirror, cardboard, and a flashlight.

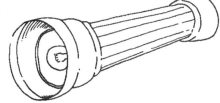

Activity: Turn out the lights and use a flashlight to reflect off the hand

mirror and onto various items in the room. As the light bounces from object to object, have family members call out those objects. Then have children each attempt to reflect the light onto specific items they saw while you were handling the light and mirror.

 Consider these questions:
- **What did the mirror do with the light from the flashlight?** (It reflected the light around the room.)

 Cover the mirror with a piece of cardboard and attempt the activity again. Then ask:
- **Now what does the mirror do?** (Nothing; it's covered by the cardboard; the light isn't reflected.)

Share: When we shine a light on a mirror, that light is reflected on other things. But if that mirror is blocked by cardboard, which represents the wrong things we do, the light isn't reflected at all. When others look at us, they see whatever we are reflecting in our lives. For example, if we're people who show God's love often, others will see that.

 Ask:
- **What would people see if they "shined a light" on you? What kinds of attitudes and behaviors would be reflected?** (Answers will vary.)
- **How does listening to God and doing what He says help us to reflect the right things?** (When we do what God wants, others see God's love; when we follow God, He is happy.)

Have family members share ideas on how they can reflect God's love to others. For example, some might say: do good things for friends; bring a friend to church; pray often; read my Bible; and so on. **Re-read** James 1:19-25 to remind children of the importance of doing God's will and reflecting His love to others.

Remove the cardboard and shine the light so it reflects off the mirror and onto each family member, one at a time. As the light settles on each person, say a word of encouragement for that person, acknowledging one way that person reflects God's love. For example, you might **say: I'm thankful that Tom shares with others—he reflects God's love by being generous;** or **I'm thankful that Cindy tells her friends about our church—she reflects God's love by bringing others to a place where they can learn about Jesus' love.**

WRAP-UP

Gather everyone in a circle and have family members take turns answering this question: **What's one thing you've learned about God today?**

Next, tell kids you've got a new "Life Slogan" you'd like to share with them.

Life Slogan: Today's Life Slogan is this: "We must hear and obey so; others may see and know." Have family members repeat the slogan two or three times to help them learn it. Then encourage them to practice saying it during the week so they can talk about it at your next family night session.

Close in Prayer: Allow time for each family member to share prayer concerns and answers to prayer. Then close your time together with prayer for each concern. Thank God for listening to and caring about us.

Remember to record your prayer requests so you can refer to them in the future as you see God answering them.

☙ 13: The Book of Life

Exploring what it takes to get into heaven

Scripture
• Revelation 20:15, 21:27

ACTIVITY OVERVIEW		
Activity	Summary	Pre-Session Prep
Activity 1: Who's in the Book?	Examine a phone book and make a list of family members' names.	You'll need a phone book, paper, and crayons or markers.
Activity 2: Guard at the Gate	Act out what it might be like to get into heaven.	You'll need a Bible and supplies for a "cloud" party.

Main Points:

—To get into heaven, your name must be in the Book of Life.

—If we accept Jesus as Savior, we'll get into heaven.

LIFE SLOGAN: "You'll be heaven bound; when your name in the Book of Life is found."

Make it your own

In the space provided below, outline the flow and add any additional ideas to guide you through the process of conducting this family night.

Prayer & Praise Items

In the space provided below, list any items you wish to pray about or give praise for during this family night session.

Journal

In the space provided below, capture a record of any fun or meaningful things which happened during this family night session.

Session Tip

We intentionally have provided more material than we would expect to be used in a single "Family Night" session. You know your family's unique interests and life circumstances best, so feel free to adapt this lesson to meet your family members' needs. Remember, short and simple is better than long and comprehensive.

WARM-UP

Open with Prayer: Begin by having a family member pray, asking God to help everyone in the family understand more about Him through this time. After prayer, review your last lesson by asking these questions:

- **What did we learn about in our last lesson?**
- **What was the Life Slogan?**
- **Have your actions changed because of what we learned? If so, how?** Encourage family members to give specific examples of how they've applied learning from the past week.

Share: Today we're going to talk about a book called the Book of Life and we're going to learn what it means to have your name written in that book.

ACTIVITY 1: Who's in the Book?

Point: To get into heaven, your name must be in the Book of Life

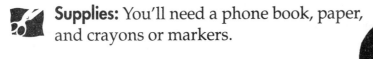 **Supplies:** You'll need a phone book, paper, and crayons or markers.

Activity: Show family members your local phone book. Explain to younger children that this book lists the names, addresses, and phone numbers of people who live in your city. Have children call out friends' names for you to look up. After you've looked at a few names, explain that you're going to create your own book of names—a book of family names. Have children help you cut, fold, and tape paper together to make a booklet. Then have them decorate the outside of the book with the words, "The [YOUR LAST NAME] Book of Family Names" and lots of colorful decorations. If possible, invite another family or two over and have each family create its own special book.

When the cover is complete, have children take turns calling out family members to list in the book. Have younger children suggest names and older children write those names in the book in colorful ways. Be sure to include grandparents, aunts, uncles, and cousins! As you think of names to include, ask family members about friends and other non-family members. They should say "they don't belong" since the book is just for family members.

When the book is complete, have family members add their own names if they haven't already. Then **share: God has a book in heaven called the Book of Life. Everyone who has accepted Jesus as Savior has his or her name written in that book. And everyone whose name is in that book will get to heaven.**

Age Adjustments

OLDER CHILDREN AND TEENAGERS may worry about friends who aren't Christians and whose names may not be in the Book of Life. Use this opportunity to share with older children, the God-ordained role of Christians in sharing the Gospel with others. Help them think of practical, relational ways to share God's love with their friends. Then, when someone you or your children know accepts Christ, celebrate together the addition to God's book of life.

? Consider these questions:
- **What does it feel like to have your name in the Book of Life?** (Exciting; special.)
- **How is our Family Book of Names like the Book of Life?** (Only certain people can be in it; only the family of Christians are listed in the Book of Life.)

Share: Our Family Book of Names lists only those people who are in our family. In a similar way, God's Book of Life only lists those people who are in the family of God. If you're a Christian—you love God and accept Jesus as Savior—your name is already in that book. It's a great feeling to know we're going to heaven because we know Jesus.

ACTIVITY 2: Guard at the Gate

Point: If we accept Jesus as Savior, we'll get into heaven.

 Supplies: You'll need a Bible and supplies for a "cloud" party.

Activity: Before this activity, secretly set up a "heaven" room in your house. Place fun "cloud" snacks such as marshmallows, cotton

candy, and ice cream on a table and hang paper clouds from the ceiling. Don't let children into this room until the proper time during this activity.

Read or summarize Revelation 20:15 and 21:27. Explain once again that, to get into heaven, a person's name must be in the Book of Life. Have one adult stand as a "guard" outside your cloud party room. Give that person a sheet of paper on which your family members' names are listed. **Share: Let's imagine that we're all standing at the gate to heaven. Here at the gate is a guard who holds a page from the Book of Life. Let's see what happens if we try to go into heaven.**

Have family members take turns going up to your guard and asking if they can enter heaven. After "checking the list," have the guard send each person into the room with the surprise party supplies. If you have done Activity 1 with other families, enjoy this as a group.

When everyone is in the room (including your guard), consider these questions as you enjoy the snacks:
- **What will it be like to see heaven for the first time?** (I will be excited; it will be hard to describe; it will be fun.)
- **What are you most looking forward to about heaven?** (No more scraped knees; I get to see Jesus; I will see my grandpa [or other relative] again.)

When you've enjoyed your snacks, close in prayer, thanking God for writing your names in the Book of Life and expecting us someday in heaven.

NOTE: If one or more family members don't yet know Jesus as Savior, this activity provides a wonderful opportunity for them to consider Christ.

WRAP-UP
Gather everyone in a circle and have family members take turns answering this question: **What's one thing you've learned about God today?**

Next, tell kids you've got a new "Life Slogan" you'd like to share with them.

Life Slogan: Today's Life Slogan is this: "You'll be heaven bound; when your name in the Book of Life is found." Have family members repeat the slogan two or three times to help them learn it. Then encourage them to practice saying it during the week so they can talk about it at

your next family night session.

Close in Prayer: Allow time for each family member to share prayer concerns and answers to prayer. Then close your time together with prayer for each concern. Thank God for listening to and caring about us.

Remember to record your prayer requests so you can refer to them in the future as you see God answering them.

Family Night
TOOL CHEST

How to Lead Your Child to Christ

SOME THINGS TO CONSIDER AHEAD OF TIME:

1. Realize that God is more concerned about your child's eternal destiny and happiness than you are. "The Lord is not slow in keeping His promise. . . . He is patient with you, not wanting anyone to perish, but everyone to come to repentance" (2 Peter 3:9).

2. Pray specifically beforehand that God will give you insights and wisdom in dealing with each child on his or her maturity level.

3. Don't use terms like "take Jesus into your heart," "dying and going to hell," and "accepting Christ as your personal Savior." Children are either too literal ("How does Jesus breathe in my heart?") or the words are too clichéd and trite for their understanding.

4. Deal with each child alone, and don't be in a hurry. Make sure he or she understands. Discuss. Take your time.

A FEW CAUTIONS:

1. When drawing children to Himself, Jesus said for others to "allow" them to come to Him (see Mark 10:14). Only with adults did He use the term "compel" (see Luke 14:23). Do not compel children.

2. Remember that unless the Holy Spirit is speaking to the child, there will be no genuine heart experience of regeneration. Parents, don't get caught up in the idea that Jesus will return the day before you were going to speak to your child about salvation and that it will be too late. Look at God's character— He *is* love! He is not dangling your child's soul over hell. Wait on God's timing.

    Pray with faith, believing. Be concerned, but don't push.

THE PLAN:

1. **God loves you.** Recite John 3:16 with your child's name in place of "the world."

2. **Show the child his or her need of a Savior.**

   a. Deal with sin carefully. There is one thing that cannot enter heaven—sin.

   b. Be sure your child knows what sin is. Ask him to name some (things common to children—lying, sassing, disobeying, etc.). Sin is doing or thinking anything wrong according to God's Word. It is breaking God's Law.

   c. Ask the question "Have you sinned?" If the answer is no, do not continue. Urge him to come and talk to you again when he does feel that he has sinned. Dismiss him. You may want to have prayer first, however, thanking God "for this young child who is willing to do what is right." Make it easy for him to talk to you again, but do not continue. Do not say, "Oh, yes, you have too sinned!" and then name some. With children, wait for God's conviction.

   d. If the answer is yes, continue. He may even give a personal illustration of some sin he has done recently or one that has bothered him.

   e. Tell him what God says about sin: We've all sinned ("There is no one righteous, not even one," Rom. 3:10). And because of that sin, we can't get to God ("For the wages of sin is death . . . " Rom. 6:23). So He had to come to us (". . . but the gift of God is eternal life in Christ Jesus our Lord," Rom. 6:23).

   f. Relate God's gift of salvation to Christmas gifts—we don't earn them or pay for them; we just accept them and are thankful for them.

3. **Bring the child to a definite decision.**

   a. Christ must be received if salvation is to be possessed.

   b. Remember, do not force a decision.

   c. Ask the child to pray out loud in her own words. Give her some things she could say if she seems unsure. Now be prepared for a blessing! (It is best to avoid having the child repeat a memorized prayer after you. Let her think, and make it personal.)*

d. After salvation has occurred, pray for her out loud. This is a good way to pronounce a blessing on her.

4. **Lead your child into assurance.**

Show him that he will have to keep his relationship open with God through repentance and forgiveness (just like with his family or friends), but that God will always love him ("Never will I leave you; never will I forsake you," Heb. 13:5).

* If you wish to guide your child through the prayer, here is some suggested language.

"Dear God, I know that I am a sinner [have child name specific sins he or she acknowledged earlier, such as lying, stealing, disobeying, etc.]. I know that Jesus died on the cross to pay for all my sins. I ask You to forgive me of my sins. I believe that Jesus died for me and rose from the dead, and I accept Him as my Savior. Thank You for loving me. In Jesus' name. Amen."

Cumulative Topical Index

TOPIC	SCRIPTURE	WHAT YOU'LL NEED	WHERE TO FIND IT
The Acts of the Sinful Nature and the Fruit of the Spirit	Gal. 5:19-26	3x5 cards or paper, markers, and tape	IFN, p. 43
Adding Value to Money through Saving Takes Time	Matt. 6:19-21	Supplies for making cookies and a Bible	MMK, p. 89
All Have Sinned	Rom. 3:23	Raw eggs, bucket of water	BCB, p. 89
All of Our Plans Should Match God's	Ps. 139:1-18	Paper, pencils, markers, or crayons	MMK, p. 73
Avoid Things That Keep Us from Growing	Eph. 4:14-15; Heb. 5:11-14	Seeds, plants at various stages of growth or a garden or nursery to tour, Bible	CCQ, p. 77
Bad Company Corrupts Good Character	1 Cor. 15:33	Small ball, string, slips of paper, pencil, yarn or masking tape, Bible	IFN, p. 103
Be Thankful for Good Friends		Bible, art supplies, markers	IFN, p. 98
Being Content with What We Have	Phil. 4:11-13	Bible	CCQ, p. 17
Being Diligent Means Working Hard and Well	Gen. 39–41	Bible, paper, a pencil and other supplies depending on jobs chosen	MMK, p. 64
Being a Faithful Steward Means Managing God's Gifts Wisely	1 Peter 4:10; Luke 19:12-26	Graham crackers, peanut butter, thin stick pretzels, small marshmallows, and M & Ms®	MMK, p. 18
Being Jealous Means Wanting Things Other People Have	Gen. 37:4-5	Different size boxes of candy or other treats, and a Bible	OTS, p. 39
Being with God in Heaven Is Worth More than Anything Else	Matt. 13:44-46	Hershey's kisses candies, a Bible	NTS, p. 24
Budgeting Means Making a Plan for Using Our Money	Jud. 6–7	Table, large sheets or paper, and markers or crayons	MMK, p. 79

TOPIC	SCRIPTURE	WHAT YOU'LL NEED	WHERE TO FIND IT
Budgeting Means the Money Coming in Has to Equal the Money Going Out	Luke 14:28-35; Jud. 6–7	Supply of beans, paper, pencil, and Bible	MMK, p. 80
Change Helps Us Grow and Mature	Rom. 8:28-39	Bible	WLS, p. 39
Change Is Good	1 Kings 17:8-16	Jar or box for holding change, colored paper, tape, markers, Bible	MMK, p. 27
Christ Is Who We Serve	Col. 3:23-24	Paper, scissors, pens	IFN, p. 50
The Christmas Story Is about Jesus' Birth	Luke 2, Matt. 2	Styrofoam cones and balls of various sizes, a large box, markers or paints, tape, a Bible	NTS, p. 47
Christians Should Be Joyful Each Day	James 3:22-23; Ps. 118:24	Small plastic bottle, cork to fit bottle opening, water, vinegar, paper towel, Bible	CCQ, p. 67
Commitment and Hard Work Are Needed to Finish Strong	Gen. 6:5-22	Jigsaw puzzle, Bible	CCQ, p. 83
The Consequence of Sin Is Death	Ps. 19:1-6	Dominoes	BCB, p. 57
Contentment Is the Secret to Happiness	Matt. 6:33	Package of candies, a Bible	MMK, p. 51
Creation	Gen. 1:1; Ps. 19:1-6; Rom. 1:20	Nature book or video, Bible	IFN, p. 17
David and Bathsheba	2 Sam. 11:1–12:14	Bible	BCB, p. 90
Description of Heaven	Rev. 21:3-4, 10-27	Bible, drawing supplies	BCB, p. 76
Difficulty Can Help Us Grow	Jer. 32:17; Luke 18:27	Bible, card game like Old Maid or Crazy Eights	CCQ, p. 33
Discipline and Training Make Us Stronger	Prov. 4:23	Narrow doorway, Bible	CCQ, p. 103
Do Not Give In to Those Around You	Matt. 14:6-12; Luke 23:13-25	Empty one two-liter plastic bottles, eye-dropper, water, a Bible	SS, p.21

TOPIC	SCRIPTURE	WHAT YOU'LL NEED	WHERE TO FIND IT
Don't Be Distracted by Unimportant Things	Matt. 14:22-32	One marked penny, lots of unmarked pennies, a wrapped gift for each child, a Bible	NTS, p. 35
Don't Be Yoked with Unbelievers	2 Cor. 16:17–17:1	Milk, food coloring	IFN, p. 105
Don't Give Respect Based on Material Wealth	Eph. 6:1-8; 1 Peter 2:13-17; Ps. 119:17; James 2:1-2; 1 Tim. 4:12	Large sheet of paper, tape, a pen, Bible	IFN, p. 64
Dorcas Made Clothes and Did Good Things	Acts 9:36-42	Large pillowcases, fabric markers, scissors, a Bible	NTS, p. 71
Easter Was God's Plan for Jesus	John 3:16; Rom. 3:23; 6:23	Paper and pencils or pens, materials to make a large cross, and a Bible	HFN, p. 27
Equality Does Not Mean Contentment	Matt. 20:1-16	Money or candy bars, tape recorder or radio, Bible	WLS, p. 21
Even if We're Not in the Majority, We May Be Right	2 Tim. 3:12-17	Piece of paper, pencil, water	CCQ, p. 95
Every Day Is a Gift from God	Prov. 16:9	Bible	CCQ, p. 69
Evil Hearts Say Evil Words	Prov. 15:2-8; Luke 6:45; Eph. 4:29	Bible, small mirror	IFN, p. 79
Family Members Ought to Be Loyal to Each Other	The Book of Ruth	Shoebox, two pieces of different colored felt, seven pipe cleaners (preferably of different colors)	OTS, p. 67
The Fruit of the Spirit	Gal. 5:22-23; Luke 3:8; Acts 26:20	Blindfold and Bible	BCB, p. 92
God Allows Testing to Help Us Mature	James 1:2-4	Bible	BCB, p. 44
God Became a Man So We Could Understand His Love	John 14:9-10	A pet of some kind, and a Bible	HFN, p. 85
God Can Clean Our Guilty Consciences	1 John 1:9	Small dish of bleach, dark piece of material, Bible	WLS, p. 95
God Can Do the Impossible	John 6:1-14	Bible, sturdy plank (6 or more inches wide and 6 to 8 feet long), a brick or similar object, snack of fish and crackers	CCQ, p. 31

TOPIC	SCRIPTURE	WHAT YOU'LL NEED	WHERE TO FIND IT
God Can Give Us Strength		Musical instruments (or pots and pans with wooden spoons) and a snack	OTS, p. 52
God Can Guide Us Away from Satan's Traps	Ps. 119:9-11; Prov. 3:5-6	Ten or more inexpensive mousetraps, pencil, blindfold, Bible	WLS, p. 72
God Can Help Us Knock Sin Out of Our Lives	Ps. 32:1-5; 1 John 1:9	Heavy drinking glass, pie tin, small slips of paper, pencils, large raw egg, cardboard tube from a roll of toilet paper, broom, masking tape, Bible	WLS, p. 53
God Can Use Us in Unique Ways to Accomplish His Plans		Strings of cloth, clothespins or strong tape, "glow sticks" or small flashlights	OTS, p. 63
God Cares for Us Even in Hard Times	Job 1–2; 42	Bible	WLS, p. 103
God Chose to Make Dads (or Moms) as a Picture of Himself	Gen. 1:26-27	Large sheets of paper, pencils, a bright light, a picture of your family, a Bible	HFN, p. 47
God Created the Heavens and the Earth	Gen. 1	Small tent or sheet and a rope, Christmas lights, two buckets (one with water), a coffee can with dirt, a tape recorder and cassette, and a flashlight	OTS, p. 17
God Created Us	Isa. 45:9, 64:8; Ps. 139:13	Bible and video of potter with clay	BCB, p. 43
God Created the World, Stars, Plants, Animals, and People	Gen. 1	Play dough or clay, safe shaping or cutting tools, a Bible	OTS, p. 19
God Doesn't Want Us to Worry	Matt. 6:25-34; Phil. 4:6-7; Ps. 55:22	Bible, paper, pencils	CCQ, p. 39
God Forgives Those Who Confess Their Sins	1 John 1:9	Sheets of paper, tape, Bible	BCB, p. 58
God Gave Jesus a Message for Us	John 1:14,18; 8:19; 12:49-50	Goldfish in water or bug in jar, water	BCB, p. 66
God Gives and God Can Take Away	Luke 12:13-21	Bible, timer with bell or buzzer, large bowl of small candies, smaller bowl for each child	CCQ, p. 15

AN INTRODUCTION TO FAMILY NIGHTS
= IFN

BASIC CHRISTIAN BELIEFS
= BCB

CHRISTIAN CHARACTER QUALITIES
= CCQ

WISDOM LIFE SKILLS
= WLS

MONEY MATTERS FOR KIDS
= MMK

HOLIDAYS FAMILY NIGHT
= HFN

BIBLE STORIES FOR PRESCHOOLERS (OLD TESTAMENT)
= OTS

SIMPLE SCIENCE
= SS

BIBLE STORIES FOR PRESCHOOLERS (NEW TESTAMENT)
= NTS

TOPIC	SCRIPTURE	WHAT YOU'LL NEED	WHERE TO FIND IT
God Gives Us the Skills We Need to Do What He Asks of Us		Materials to make a sling (cloth, shoe-strings), plastic golf balls or marshmal-lows, stuffed animals	OTS, p. 73
God Is Holy	Ex. 3:1-6	Masking tape, baby powder or corn starch, broom, Bible	IFN, p. 31
God Is Invisible, Powerful, and Real	John 1:18, 4:24; Luke 24:36-39	Balloons, balls, refrigerator magnets, Bible	IFN, p. 15
God Is the Source of Our Strength	Jud. 16	Oversized sweat-shirt, balloons, mop heads or other items to use as wigs, items to stack to make pillars, a Bible	OTS, p. 61
God Is Our Only Source of Strength	Isa. 40:29-31	Straws, fresh baking potatoes, a Bible	SS, p.33
God Is with Us	Ex. 25:10-22; Deut. 10:1-5; Josh. 3:14-17; 1 Sam. 3:3; 2 Sam. 6:12-15	A large cardboard box, two broom han-dles, a utility knife, strong tape, gold spray paint, and a Bible	OTS, p. 49
God Keeps His Promises	Gen. 6–9:16	Plastic coffee can lid, flashlight, bubble solution, straw, a Bible	SS, p.75
God Keeps His Promises	Gen. 9:13, 15	Sheets of colored cel-lophane, cardboard, scissors, tape, a Bible, a lamp or large flashlight	OTS, p. 25
God Knew His Plans for Us	Jer. 29:11	Two puzzles and a Bible	BCB, p. 19
God Knew Moses Would Be Found by Pharaoh's Daughter	Ex. 2:1-10	A doll or stuffed animal, a basket, and a blanket	OTS, p. 43
God Knows All about Us	Ps. 139:2-4; Matt. 10:30	3x5 cards, a pen	BCB, p. 17
God Knows Everything	Isa. 40:13-14; Eph. 4:1-6	Bible	IFN, p. 15
God Knows the Plan for Our Lives	Rom. 8:28	Three different 25–50 piece jigsaw puzzles, Bible	WLS, p. 101
God Looks at the Heart	1 Sam. 16:7; Gal. 2:6	4 cans of pop (2 regular and 2 diet), 1 large tub, duct tape, water, a Bible	SS, p. 81

TOPIC	SCRIPTURE	WHAT YOU'LL NEED	WHERE TO FIND IT
God Looks beyond the Mask and into Our Hearts		Costumes	HFN, p. 65
God Loves and Protects Us	Matt. 6:26-27	One or two raw eggs, a sink or bucket, a Bible	SS, p. 15
God Loves Us So Much, He Sent Jesus	John 3:16; Eph. 2:8-9	I.O.U. for each family member	IFN, p. 34
God Made Our Family Unique by Placing Each of Us in It		Different color paint for each family member, toothpicks or paintbrushes to dip into paint, white paper, Bible	BCB, p. 110
God Made Us		Building blocks, such as Tinkertoys, Legos, or K'nex	HFN, p. 15
God Made Us in His Image	Gen. 1:24-27	Play dough or clay and Bible	BCB, p. 24
God Never Changes	Ecc. 3:1-8; Heb. 13:8	Paper, pencils, Bible	WLS, p. 37
God Owns Everything; He Gives Us Things to Manage		Large sheet of poster board or newsprint and colored markers	MMK, p. 17
God Provides a Way Out of Temptation	1 Cor. 10:12-13; James 1:13-14; 4:7; 1 John 2:15-17	Bible	IFN, p. 88
God Sees Who We Really Are—We Can Never Fool Him	1 Sam. 16:7	Construction paper, scissors, crayons or markers, a hat or bowl, and a Bible	HFN, p. 66
God Strengthens Us and Protects Us from Satan	2 Thes. 3:3; Ps. 18:2-3	Two un-inflated black balloons, water, a candle, matches, a Bible	SS, p. 16
God Teaches Us about Love through Others	1 Cor. 13	Colored paper, markers, crayons, scissors, tape or glue, and a Bible	HFN, p. 22
God Used Plagues to Tell Pharaoh to Let Moses and His People Go	Ex. 7–12	A clear glass, red food coloring, water, and a Bible	OTS, p. 44
God Uses Many Ways to Get Our Attention	Dan. 5	Large sheets of paper or poster board, tape, finger-paint, and a Bible	OTS, p. 79
God Wants Our Best Effort in All We Do	Col. 3:23-24	Children's blocks or a large supply of cardboard boxes	MMK, p. 63

Family Night
TOOL CHEST

AN INTRODUCTION TO FAMILY NIGHTS
= IFN

BASIC CHRISTIAN BELIEFS
= BCB

CHRISTIAN CHARACTER QUALITIES
= CCQ

WISDOM LIFE SKILLS
= WLS

MONEY MATTERS FOR KIDS
= MMK

HOLIDAYS FAMILY NIGHT
= HFN

BIBLE STORIES FOR PRESCHOOLERS (OLD TESTAMENT)
= OTS

SIMPLE SCIENCE
= SS

BIBLE STORIES FOR PRESCHOOLERS (NEW TESTAMENT)
= NTS

TOPIC	SCRIPTURE	WHAT YOU'LL NEED	WHERE TO FIND IT
God Wants a Passionate Relationship with Us	Rev. 3:16	Pans of hot, cold, and lukewarm water, hot and cold drinks	SS, p. 69
God Wants Us to Be Diligent in Our Work	Prov. 6:6-11; 1 Thes. 4:11-12	Video about ants or picture books or encyclopedia, Bible	CCQ, p. 55
God Wants Us to Get Closer to Him	James 4:8; 1 John 4:7-12	Hidden Bibles, clues to find them	BCB, p. 33
God Wants Us to Give to Others in Love		Candy	NTS, p. 54
God Wants Us to Glorify Him	Ps. 24:1; Luke 12:13-21	Paper, pencils, Bible	WLS, p. 47
God Wants Us to Reflect His Word	James 1:19-25	Bible, hand mirror, cardboard, a flashlight	NTS, p. 84
God Wants Us to Work and Be Helpful	2 Thes. 3:6-15	Several undone chores, Bible	CCQ, p. 53
God Will Never Leave Us or Forsake Us	Matt. 28:20	Long sheet of paper, pencil, scissors, tape or glue, a Bible	SS, p. 76
God Will Send the Holy Spirit	John 14:23-26; 1 Cor. 2:12	Flashlights, small treats, Bible	IFN, p. 39
God Will Separate Those Who Believe in Jesus from Those Who Don't	Matt. 13:47-49; John 3:16	Large box, crayons or markers, a large bath towel, candy-size rocks, candy, wax paper, a Bible	NTS, p. 29
God Will Separate Those Who Love Him from Those Who Don't	Matt. 25:31-46	Coarse salt, ground pepper, plastic spoon, wool cloth, a Bible	SS, p. 64
God's Covenant with Noah	Gen. 8:13-21; 9:8-17	Bible, paper, crayons or markers	BCB, p. 52
A Good Friend Encourages Us to Do What Jesus Would Do	Ecc. 4:9-12	Strips of cardboard, books, 50 pennies, a Bible	SS, p. 82
Guarding the Gate to Our Minds	Prov. 4:13; 2 Cor. 11:3; Phil. 4:8	Bible, poster board for each family member, old maga-zines, glue, scissors, markers	CCQ, p. 23
The Holy Spirit Helps Us	Eph. 1:17; John 14:15-17; Acts 1:1-11; Eph. 3:16-17; Rom. 8:26-27; 1 Cor. 2:11-16	Bible	BCB, p. 99

TOPIC	SCRIPTURE	WHAT YOU'LL NEED	WHERE TO FIND IT
The Holy Spirit Helps Us to Be a Light in the Dark World	Matt. 5:14-16; 1 Tim. 2:1-4	Wintergreen or Cryst-O-Mint Lifesavers, a Bible	SS, p. 40
Honesty Means Being Sure We Tell the Truth and Are Fair	Prov. 10:9; 11:3; 12:5; 14:2; 28:13	A bunch of coins and a Bible	MMK, p. 58
Honor the Holy Spirit, Don't Block Him	1 John 4:4; 1 Cor. 6:19-20	Bible, blow-dryer or vacuum cleaner with exit hose, a Ping-Pong ball	CCQ, p. 47
Honor Your Parents	Ex. 20:12	Paper, pencil, treats, umbrella, soft objects, masking tape, pen, Bible	IFN, p. 55
How Big Is an Ark?		Large open area, buckets of water, cans of animal food, bags of dog food, and four flags	OTS, p. 24
If We Accept Jesus as Savior, We'll Get into Heaven	Rev. 20:15, 21:27	Bible, marshmallows, cotton candy, ice cream	NTS, p. 90
If We Confess Our Sins, Jesus Will Forgive Us	Heb. 12:1; 1 John 1:9	Magic slate, candies, paper, pencils, bathrobe ties or soft rope, items to weigh someone down, and a Bible	HFN, p. 28
Investing and Saving Adds Value to Money	Prov. 21:20	Two and a half dollars for each family member	MMK, p. 87
It Is Important to Spend Time Praising God	Ps. 66:1; 81:1; 95:1; 98:4; 100:1	Plastic straws, scissors, a Bible	SS, p. 52
It's Better to Follow the Truth	Rom. 1:25; Prov. 2:1-5	Second set of clues, box of candy or treats, Bible	WLS, p. 86
It's Better to Wait for Something Than to Borrow Money to Buy It	2 Kings 4:1-7; Prov. 22:7	Magazines, advertisements, paper, a pencil, Bible	MMK, p. 103
It's Difficult to Be a Giver When You're a Debtor		Pennies or other coins	MMK, p. 105
It's Easy to Follow a Lie, but It Leads to Disappointment		Clues as described in lesson, empty box	WLS, p. 85
The Importance of Your Name Being Written in the Book of Life	Rev. 20:11-15; 21:27	Bible, phone book, access to other books with family name	BCB, p. 74

TOPIC	SCRIPTURE	WHAT YOU'LL NEED	WHERE TO FIND IT
It's Important to Listen to Jesus' Message		Bible	BCB, p. 68
It's Not Always Easy to Do What Jesus Wants Us to Do	Matt. 7:13	Toy blocks, a narrow board, two cinder blocks, a Bible	NTS, p. 17
It's Not Easy to Break a Pattern of Sin	James 1:12-15	Paper, pan, water, a Bible	SS, p. 63
Jesus Came to Die for Our Sins	Rom. 5:8	A large piece of cardboard, markers, scissors, tape, and a Bible	HFN, p. 91
Jesus Came to Give Us Eternal Life	Mark 16:12-14	A calculator, a calendar, a sheet of paper, and a pencil	HFN, p. 91
Jesus Came to Teach Us about God	John 1:14, 18	Winter clothing, bread crumbs, a Bible	HFN, p. 92
Jesus Came to Show Us How Much God Loves Us	John 3:16	Supplies to make an Advent wreath, and a Bible	HFN, p. 89
Jesus Comes to Find Us When We Are Lost	Luke 15:1-7	Bible, blindfolds	NTS, p. 61
Jesus Cried Just Like We Do	John 11	Children's Bible storybook, a Bible, or video, *The Easter Promise*	NTS, p. 65
Jesus Died for Our Sins	Luke 22:1-6; Mark 14:12-26; Luke 22:47-54; Luke 22:55-62; Matt. 27:1-10; Matt. 27:11-31; Luke 23:26-34	Seven plastic eggs, slips of paper with Scripture verses, and a Bible	HFN, p. 33
Jesus Dies on the Cross	John 14:6	6-foot 2x4, 3-foot 2x4, hammers, nails, Bible	IFN, p. 33
Jesus Has Power over Death		Toilet paper rolls	NTS, p. 66
Jesus Promises Us New Bodies and a New Home in Heaven	Phil. 3:20-21; Luke 24:36-43; Rev. 21:1-4	Ingredients for making pumpkin pie, and a Bible	HFN, p. 61
Jesus Took Our Sins to the Cross and Freed Us from Being Bound Up in Sin	Rom. 6:23, 5:8; 6:18	Soft rope or heavy yarn, a watch with a second hand, thread, and a Bible	HFN, p. 53
Jesus Took the Punishment We Deserve	Rom. 6:23; John 3:16; Rom. 5:8-9	Bathrobe, list of bad deeds	IFN, p. 26

TOPIC	SCRIPTURE	WHAT YOU'LL NEED	WHERE TO FIND IT
Jesus Wants Us to Do the Right Thing			NTS, p. 18
Jesus Was Victorious Over Death and Sin	Luke 23:35-43; Luke 23:44-53; Matt. 27:59-61; Luke 23:54–24:12	Five plastic eggs—four with Scripture verses, and a Bible	HFN, p. 36
Jesus Washes His Followers' Feet	John 13:1-17	Bucket of warm soapy water, towels, Bible	IFN, p. 63
Joshua and the Battle of Jericho	Josh. 1:16-18; 6:1-21	Paper, pencil, dots on paper that, when connected, form a star	IFN, p. 57
Knowing God's Word Helps Us Know What Stand to Take	2 Tim. 3:1-5	Current newspaper, Bible	CCQ, p. 93
Look to God, Not Others	Phil. 4:11-13	Magazines or newspapers, a chair, several pads of small yellow stickies, Bible	WLS, p. 24
Love Is Unselfish	1 Cor. 13	A snack and a Bible	HFN, p. 21
Love Means Putting Others' Needs above Our Own	Luke 10:25-37	Children's Bible storybook, two equal-length strips of wood, paper, marker, costumes, a Bible	NTS, p. 53
Loving Money Is Wrong	1 Tim. 6:6-10	Several rolls of coins, masking tape, Bible	WLS, p. 45
Lying Can Hurt People	Acts 5:1-11	Two pizza boxes—one empty and one with a fresh pizza—and a Bible	MMK, p. 57
Meeting Goals Requires Planning	Prov. 3:5-6	Paper, scissors, pencils, a treat, a Bible	MMK, p. 71
Moms Are Special and Important to Us and to God	Prov. 24:3-4	Confetti, streamers, a comfortable chair, a wash basin with warm water, two cloths, and a Bible	HFN, p. 41
Moms Model Jesus' Love When They Serve Gladly	2 Tim. 1:4-7	Various objects depending on chosen activity and a Bible	HFN, p. 42
The More We Know God, the More We Know His Voice	John 10:1-6	Bible	BCB, p. 35
Nicodemus Asks Jesus about Being Born Again	John 3:7, 50-51; 19:39-40	Bible, paper, pencil, costume	BCB, p. 81

Family Night
TOOL CHEST

AN INTRODUCTION TO FAMILY NIGHTS
= IFN

BASIC CHRISTIAN BELIEFS
= BCB

CHRISTIAN CHARACTER QUALITIES
= CCQ

WISDOM LIFE SKILLS
= WLS

MONEY MATTERS FOR KIDS
= MMK

HOLIDAYS FAMILY NIGHT
= HFN

BIBLE STORIES FOR PRESCHOOLERS (OLD TESTAMENT)
= OTS

SIMPLE SCIENCE
= SS

BIBLE STORIES FOR PRESCHOOLERS (NEW TESTAMENT)
= NTS

TOPIC	SCRIPTURE	WHAT YOU'LL NEED	WHERE TO FIND IT
Noah Obeyed God When He Built the Ark	Gen. 6:14-16	A large refrigerator box, markers or paints, self-adhesive paper, stuffed animals, a Bible, utility knife	OTS, p. 23
Nothing Is Impossible When It Is in God's Will	Matt. 21:28	Hard-boiled egg, butter, glass bottle, paper, matches, a Bible	SS, p. 34
Obedience Has Good Rewards		Planned outing everyone will enjoy, directions on 3x5 cards, number cards	IFN, p. 59
Obey God First		Paper, markers, scissors, and blindfolds	OTS, p. 80
Only a Relationship with God Can Fill Our Need	Isa. 55:1-2	Doll that requires batteries, batteries for the doll, dollar bill, pictures of a house, an expensive car, and a pretty woman or handsome man, Bible	WLS, p. 62
Our Actions Should Mirror God, Not the World	Rom. 12:2	Regular glass, dried peas, a wine glass, a pie tin, water, a Bible	SS, p. 57
Our Conscience Helps Us Know Right from Wrong	Rom. 2:14-15	Foods with a strong smell, blindfold, Bible	WLS, p. 93
Our Minds Should Be Filled with Good, Not Evil	Phil 4:8; Ps. 119:9, 11	Bible, bucket of water, several large rocks	CCQ, p. 26
Our Tongue Is Powerful and Should Be Used to Glorify God	James 3:5-8	Squirt gun, pie pan, Pop Rocks candy, a Bible	SS, p. 51
Parable of the Talents	Matt. 25:14-30	Bible	IFN, p. 73
Parable of the Vine and Branches	John 15:1-8	Tree branch, paper, pencils, Bible	IFN, p. 95
People Came to See Jesus and Bring Him Gifts	Luke 2, Matt. 2	Styrofoam cones and balls of various sizes, a large box, markers or paints, tape, a Bible	NTS, p. 48
People, Like Plants, Need Good Soil to Grow	Mark 4:3-8, 13-20	Cake pan, aluminum foil, small stones, seeds, toothpicks, potting soil, a Bible	NTS, p. 41

TOPIC	SCRIPTURE	WHAT YOU'LL NEED	WHERE TO FIND IT
People Look at Outside Appearance, but God Looks at the Heart	1 Sam. 17	Slings from activity on p. 73, plastic golf balls or marshmallows, a tape measure, cardboard, markers, and a Bible	OTS, p. 75
People Who Have the Gift of Hospitality Open Their Homes and Serve Others		Snacks and supplies for a nice meal	NTS, p. 78
Persecution Brings a Reward		Bucket, bag of ice, marker, one-dollar bill	WLS, p. 32
Planning Helps Us Finish Strong	Phil. 3:10-14	Flight map on p. 86, paper, pencils, Bible	CCQ, p. 85
Pray, Endure, and Be Glad When We're Persecuted	Matt. 5:11-12, 44; Rom. 12:14; 1 Cor. 4:12	Notes, Bible, candle or flashlight, dark small space	WLS, p. 29
Priscilla Had the Gift of Hospitality	Acts 18:1-4, 18-26; Rom. 16:3-5	Large sheet, rope, clothespins, a Bible	NTS, p. 77
Putting God First Builds a Solid Relationship	Mark 6:35; Luke 4:16; Mark 13:31; Luke 12:31	Wide-mouth glass jar, large rocks, sand, water, permanent marker, a Bible	SS, p. 70
Remember All God Has Done for You	Ex. 25:1; 16:34; Num. 17:10; Deut. 31:26	Ark of the covenant from p. 49, cardboard or Styrofoam, crackers, a stick, and a Bible	OTS, p. 51
Remember What God Has Done for You	Gen. 12:7-8; 13:18; 22:9	Bricks or large rocks, paint, and a Bible	OTS, p. 31
The Responsibilities of Families	Eph. 5:22-33; 6:1-4	Photo albums, Bible	BCB, p. 101
Satan Looks for Ways to Trap Us	Luke 4:1-13	Cardboard box, string, stick, small ball, Bible	WLS, p. 69
Self-control Helps Us Resist the Enemy	1 Peter 5:8-9; 1 Peter 2:11-12	Blindfold, watch or timer, feather or other "tickly" item, Bible	CCQ, p. 101
Serve One Another in Love	Gal. 5:13	Bag of small candies, at least three per child	IFN, p. 47
Share God's Love with Others So They Can Join Us in Heaven		Rocks, plastic bags, paper, pencils	NTS, p. 30

Family Night
TOOL CHEST

AN INTRODUCTION TO FAMILY NIGHTS
= IFN

BASIC CHRISTIAN BELIEFS
= BCB

CHRISTIAN CHARACTER QUALITIES
= CCQ

WISDOM LIFE SKILLS
= WLS

MONEY MATTERS FOR KIDS
= MMK

HOLIDAYS FAMILY NIGHT
= HFN

BIBLE STORIES FOR PRESCHOOLERS (OLD TESTAMENT)
= OTS

SIMPLE SCIENCE
= SS

BIBLE STORIES FOR PRESCHOOLERS (NEW TESTAMENT)
= NTS

TOPIC	SCRIPTURE	WHAT YOU'LL NEED	WHERE TO FIND IT
Sin and Busyness Interfere with Our Prayers	Luke 10:38-42; Ps. 46:10; Matt. 5:23-24; 1 Peter 3:7	Bible, two paper cups, two paper clips, long length of fishing line	CCQ, p. 61
Sin Separates Humanity	Gen. 3:1-24	Bible, clay creations, piece of hardened clay or play dough	BCB, p. 25
Some Places Aren't Open to Everyone		Book or magazine with "knock-knock" jokes	BCB, p. 73
Some Things in Life Are Out of Our Control		Blindfolds	BCB, p. 41
Sometimes God Surprises Us with Great Things	Gen. 15:15	Large sheet of poster board, straight pins or straightened paper clips, a flashlight, and a Bible	OTS, p. 32
Sometimes We Face Things That Seem Impossible		Bunch of cardboard boxes or blocks	OTS, p. 55
Stand Strong in the Lord	Prov. 1:8-10; 12:3	A jar, string, chair, fan, small weight, a Bible	SS, p. 22
Temptation Takes Our Eyes Off God		Fishing pole, items to catch, timer, Bible	IFN, p. 85
Test What the World Offers for Consistency with Jesus' Teachings	1 John 4:1	Candle, apple, almond, a Bible	SS, p. 58
There Is a Difference between Needs and Wants	Prov. 31:16; Matt. 6:21	Paper, pencils, glasses of drinking water, a soft drink	MMK, p. 95
Things That Are Important to Us Don't Always Cost a Lot of Money		Stuffed toy, candy bar, toys, etc.	NTS, p. 23
Those Who Don't Believe Are Foolish	Ps. 44:1	Ten small pieces of paper, pencil, Bible	IFN, p. 19
Tithing Means Giving One-Tenth Back to God	Gen. 28:10-22; Ps. 3:9-10	All family members need ten similar items each, a Bible	MMK, p. 33
To Get to Heaven, Your Name Must Be in the Book of Life		Phone book, paper, crayons or markers	NTS, p. 89
The Tongue Is Small but Powerful	James 3:3-12	Video, news magazine or picture book showing devastation of fire, match, candle, Bible	IFN, p. 77

TOPIC	SCRIPTURE	WHAT YOU'LL NEED	WHERE TO FIND IT
The Treasure of a Thankful Heart Is Contentment	Eph. 5:20	3x5 cards, pencils, fun prizes, and a Bible	HFN, p. 72
Trials Help Us Grow	James 1:2-4	Sugar cookie dough, cookie cutters, baking sheets, miscellaneous baking supplies, Bible	WLS, p. 15
Trials Test How We've Grown	James 1:12	Bible	WLS, p. 17
Trust Is Important	Matt. 6:25-34	Each person needs an item he or she greatly values	MMK, p. 25
We All Have Weaknesses and Will Be Attacked by Satan	1 Kings 11:3-4; 2 Cor. 12:9-10	Two pieces of plain white paper, a pencil, a Bible	SS, p. 28
We All Sin	Rom. 3:23	Target and items to throw	IFN, p. 23
We Are a Family for Life, Forever	Ruth 1:4	Shoebox; scissors; paper or cloth; magnets; photos of family members, friends, others; and a Bible	OTS, p. 68
We Are Made in God's Image	Gen. 2:7; Ps. 139:13-16	Paper bags, candies, a Bible, supplies for making gingerbread cookies	HFN, p. 17
We Become a New Creation When Jesus Comes into Our Hearts	Matt. 23:25-28; Rev. 3:20; 2 Cor. 5:17; Eph. 2:10; 2 Cor. 4:7-10; Matt. 5:14-16; 2 Cor. 4:6	Pumpkin, newspaper, sharp knife, a spoon, a candle, matches, and a Bible	HFN, p. 59
We Can Communicate with Each Other			BCB, p. 65
We Can Do Good Things for Others	1 Cor. 13:4	Newsprint or a large sheet of paper, markers or crayons, children's clothing, money to buy new clothes, a Bible	NTS, p. 72
We Can Fight the Temptation to Want More Stuff	Matt. 4:1-11; Heb. 13:5	Television, paper, a pencil, Bible	MMK, p. 49
We Can Give Joyfully to Others	Luke 10:25-37	Bible, soft yarn	MMK, p. 41
We Can Help Each Other	Prov. 27:17	Masking tape, bowl of unwrapped candies, rulers, yardsticks, or dowel rods	BCB, p. 110

Family Night
TOOL CHEST

AN INTRODUCTION TO FAMILY NIGHTS
= IFN

BASIC CHRISTIAN BELIEFS
= BCB

CHRISTIAN CHARACTER QUALITIES
= CCQ

WISDOM LIFE SKILLS
= WLS

MONEY MATTERS FOR KIDS
= MMK

HOLIDAYS FAMILY NIGHT
= HFN

BIBLE STORIES FOR PRESCHOOLERS (OLD TESTAMENT)
= OTS

SIMPLE SCIENCE
= SS

BIBLE STORIES FOR PRESCHOOLERS (NEW TESTAMENT)
= NTS

TOPIC	SCRIPTURE	WHAT YOU'LL NEED	WHERE TO FIND IT
We Can Help People When We Give Generously	2 Cor. 6–7	Variety of supplies, depending on chosen activity	MMK, p. 43
We Can Learn about God from Mom (or Dad)		Supplies to make a collage (magazines, paper, tape or glue, scissors)	HFN, p. 49
We Can Learn and Grow from Good and Bad Situations	Gen. 37–48; Rom. 8:29	A Bible and a camera (optional)	OTS, p. 37
We Can Love by Helping Those in Need	Heb. 13:1-3		IFN, p. 48
We Can Show Love through Respecting Family Members		Paper and pen	IFN, p. 66
We Can't Hide from God		Supplies will vary	OTS, p. 85
We Can't Take Back the Damage of Our Words		Tube of toothpaste for each child, $10 bill	IFN, p. 78
We Deserve Punishment for Our Sins	Rom. 6:23	Dessert, other materials as decided	IFN, p. 24
We Give to God because We're Thankful		Supplies for a celebration dinner, also money for each family member	MMK, p. 36
We Have All We Need in Our Lives	Ecc. 3:11	Paper, pencils, Bible	WLS, p. 61
We Have a New Life in Christ	John 3:3; 2 Cor. 5:17	Video or picture book of caterpillar forming a cocoon then a butterfly, or a tadpole becoming a frog, or a seed becoming a plant	BCB, p. 93
We Have Much to Be Thankful For	1 Chron. 16:4-36	Unpopped popcorn, a bowl, supplies for popping popcorn, and a Bible	HFN, p. 79
We Know Others by Our Relationships with Them		Copies of question-naire, pencils, Bible	BCB, p. 31
We Must Be in Constant Contact with God		Blindfold	CCQ, p. 63
We Must Choose to Obey		3x5 cards or slips of paper, markers, and tape	IFN, p. 43

TOPIC	SCRIPTURE	WHAT YOU'LL NEED	WHERE TO FIND IT
We Must Either Choose Christ or Reject Christ	Matt. 12:30	Clear glass jar, cooking oil, water, spoon, Bible	CCQ, p. 96
We Must Give Thanks in All Circumstances	1 Thes. 5:18	A typical family meal, cloth strips, and a Bible	HFN, p. 77
We Must Hold Firm to Our Faith and Depend on God for Strength	Eph. 6:16	Balloons, long darts or shish kebab skewers, cooking oil, a Bible	SS, p. 27
We Must Learn How Much Responsibility We Can Handle		Building blocks, watch with second hand, paper, pencil	IFN, p. 71
We Must Listen	Prov. 1:5, 8-9; 4:1	Bible, other supplies for the task you choose	WLS, p. 77
We Must "Root" Ourselves in Jesus and Live by God's Word	Mark 4:1-24	A potted plant, light-weight cardboard, crayons, scissors, a Bible	NTS, p. 42
We Must Stay Focused on Jesus So We Don't Fall		Masking tape	NTS, p. 36
We Must Think Before We Speak	James 1:19	Bible	WLS, p. 79
We Need to Feed on God's Word to Grow in Christ	Ps. 119:105; 2 Chron. 34:31; Acts 17:11; James 1:22-25	Raisins, clear drinking glass, a two-liter bottle of clear soft drink, a Bible	SS, p. 46
We Need to Grow Closer to Jesus Each Day	Acts 9:1-18	Pitcher, lemonade mix (sugarless), sugar, dry ice, a Bible	SS, p. 45
We Need to Grow Physically, Emotionally, and Spiritually	1 Peter 2:2	Photograph albums or videos of your children at different ages, tape measure, bathroom scale, Bible	CCQ, p. 75
We Prove Who We Are When What We Do Reflects What We Say	James 1:22; 2:14-27	A bag of candy, a rope, and a Bible	HFN, p. 67
We Reap What We Sow	Gal. 6:7	Candy bar, Bible	IFN, p. 55
We Should Do What God Wants Even If We Don't Think We Can		A powerful fan, large sheet of light-weight black plastic, duct tape, and a flashlight	OTS, p. 86
We Shouldn't Value Possessions Over Everything Else	1 Tim. 6:7-8	Box is optional	CCQ, p. 18

AN INTRODUCTION TO FAMILY NIGHTS
= IFN

BASIC CHRISTIAN BELIEFS
= BCB

CHRISTIAN CHARACTER QUALITIES
= CCQ

WISDOM LIFE SKILLS
= WLS

MONEY MATTERS FOR KIDS
= MMK

HOLIDAYS FAMILY NIGHT
= HFN

BIBLE STORIES FOR PRESCHOOLERS (OLD TESTAMENT)
= OTS

SIMPLE SCIENCE
= SS

BIBLE STORIES FOR PRESCHOOLERS (NEW TESTAMENT)
= NTS

TOPIC	SCRIPTURE	WHAT YOU'LL NEED	WHERE TO FIND IT
When a Sheep Is Lost, the Shepherd Finds It		Shoebox, felt, pom pom balls	NTS, p. 58
When God Sent Jesus to Earth, God Chose Me	Luke 1:26-38; John 3:16; Matt. 14:23	Going to choose a Christmas tree or other special decoration, a Bible, and hot chocolate	HFN, p. 83
When We Accept Jesus' Gift of Salvation, We Receive the Holy Spirit	John 3:5-8	1/4-full roll of toilet paper, a blow dryer, a dowel rod, a Bible	SS, p. 39
When We Focus on What We Don't Have, We Get Unhappy	1 Tim. 6:9-10; 1 Thes. 5:18; Phil. 4:11-13	A glass, water, paper, crayons, and a Bible	HFN, p. 71
When We See Something Wrong with the Way We Act, We Should Fix It	James 1:22-24	Clothing, a large mirror, a Bible	NTS, p. 83
When We're Set Free from Sin, We Have the Freedom to Choose, and the Responsibility to Serve	Gal. 5:13-15	Candies, soft rope, and a Bible	HFN, p. 55
Wise Spending Means Getting Good Value for What We Buy	Luke 15:11-32	Money and a Bible	MMK, p. 97
With Help, Life Is a Lot Easier		Supplies to do the chore you choose	BCB, p. 101
Wolves in Sheeps' Clothing	Matt. 7:15-20	Ten paper sacks, a marker, ten small items, Bible	IFN, p. 97
Worrying Doesn't Change Anything		Board, inexpensive doorbell buzzer, a 9-volt battery, extra length of electrical wire, a large belt, assorted tools	CCQ, p. 37
You Look Like the Person in Whose Image You Are Created		Paper roll, crayons, markers, pictures of your kids and of yourself as a child	BCB, p. 23

Welcome to the Family!

Heritage Builders

Helping You Build a Family of Faith

We hope you've enjoyed this book. Heritage Builders was founded in 1995 by three fathers with a passion for the next generation. As a new ministry of Focus on the Family, Heritage Builders strives to equip, train and motivate parents to become intentional about building a strong spiritual heritage.

It's quite a challenge for busy parents to find ways to build a spiritual foundation for their families—especially in a way they enjoy and understand. Through activities and participation, children can learn biblical truth in a way they can understand, enjoy—and *remember.*

Passing along a heritage of Christian faith to your family is a parent's highest calling. Heritage Builders' goal is to encourage and empower you in this great mission with practical resources and inspiring ideas that really work— and help your children develop a lasting love for God.

***

How To Reach Us

For more information, visit our Heritage Builders Web site! Log on to **www.heritagebuilders.com** to discover new resources, sample activities, and ideas to help you pass on a spiritual heritage. To request any of these resources, simply call Focus on the Family at 1-800-A-FAMILY (1-800-232-6459) or in Canada, call 1-800-661-9800. Or send your request to Focus on the Family, Colorado Springs, CO 80995. In Canada, write Focus on the Family, P.O. Box 9800, Stn. Terminal, Vancouver, B.C. V6B 4G3

To learn more about Focus on the Family or to find out if there is an associate office in your country, please visit www. family.org

We'd love to hear from you!

Try These Heritage Builders Resources!

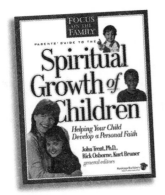

Parents' Guide to the
Spiritual Growth of Children

Building a foundation of faith in your children can be easy–
and fun!–with help from the *Parents' Guide to the Spiritual Growth
of Children*. Through simple and practical advice,
this comprehensive guide shows you how to build a
spiritual training plan for your family and it explains
what to teach your children at different ages.

Bedtime Blessings

Strengthen the precious bond between you, your child and God by making
Bedtime Blessings a special part of your evenings together. From best-selling author John
Trent, Ph.D., and Heritage Builders, this book is filled with stories, activities and blessing
prayers to help you practice the biblical model of "blessing."

My Time With God

Send your child on an amazing adventure—a self-guided tour through God's Word! *My Time
With God* shows your 8- to 12-year-old how to get to know God regularly in exciting ways.
Through 150 days' worth of fun facts and mind-boggling trivia, prayer starters, and
interesting questions, your child will discover how awesome God really is!

The Singing Bible

Children ages 2 to 7 will love *The Singing Bible*, which sets the Bible to music with over
50 fun, sing-along songs! Lead your child through Scripture by using *The Singing Bible*
to introduce the story of Jonah, the Ten Commandments and more.
This is a fun, fast-paced journey kids will remember.

. . .

Visit our Heritage Builders Web Site! Log on to
www.heritagebuilders. com to discover new resources,
sample activities, and ideas to help you pass on a spiritual heritage.
To request any of these resources, simply call Focus on the Family at
1-800-A-FAMILY (1-800-232-6459) or in Canada, call 1-800-661-9800.
Or send your request to Focus on the Family, Colorado Springs, CO
80995. In Canada, Write Focus on the Family, P.O. Box 9800,
Stn. Terminal, Vancouver, B.C. V6B 4G3.

Helping You Build a Family of Faith

Every family has a heritage—a spiritual, emotional, and social
legacy passed from one generation to the next. There are four
main areas we at Heritage Builders recommend parents consider
as they plan to pass their faith to their children:

Family Fragrance

Every family's home has a fragrance. Heritage Builders encourages parents to
create a home environment that fosters a sweet, Christ-centered AROMA
of love through Affection, Respect, Order, Merriment, and Affirmation.

Family Traditions

Whether you pass down stories, beliefs and/or customs, traditions can help
you establish a special identity for your family. Heritage Builders encourages
parents to set special "milestones" for their children to help guide them and
move them through their spiritual development.

Family Compass

Parents have the unique task of setting standards for normal,
healthy living through their attitudes, actions and beliefs. Heritage
Builders encourages parents to give their children the moral navigation
tools they need to succeed on the roads of life.

Family Moments

Creating special, teachable moments with their children is one of a parent's
most precious and sometimes, most difficult responsibilities. Heritage Builders
encourages parents to capture little moments throughout the day to teach
and impress values, beliefs, and biblical principles onto their children.

We look forward to standing alongside you as you seek to impart the Lord's
care and wisdom onto the next generation—onto your children.

Heritage
Builders
Helping You Build a Family of Faith